The Audacity Code: Coloring in Black Outside the Lines

JUANITA JOHNSON

Published by

Hybrid Global Publishing

301 E 57th Street

4th Floor

New York, NY 10022

Manufactured in the United States of America, or in the United Kingdom when distributed elsewhere.

Johnson, Juanita

The Audacity Code: Coloring in Black Outside the Lines

LCCN: 2020924735

    ISBN: 978-1-7358014-0-7

    Large print: 978-1-7358014-3-8

    eBook: 978-1-7358014-1-4

Cover design by: Jonathan Pleska

Copyediting by: Judee Light

Interior design by: Suba Murugan

Author photo by: Tina Bernard

Disclaimer: The stories depicted in this book are based on historical records. Both the author and publisher have made every effort to ensure that the information in this book was correct at press time. Neither the author or publisher assume and hereby disclaim any liability to any party for any loss, damage, or disruption caused by errors or omissions, whether such errors or omissions result from negligence, accident, or any other cause.

www.juanitabjohnson.com

DEDICATION

This book is lovingly dedicated to my mother
Betty L. Johnson, the light of my life

and to the legacies of
my father Lamar L. Kirven, Ph.D., a gifted historian
my beloved grandmother Addie K. McMarion, the family griot

and the memory of
Josie C. Bellard whose love of the African-American community continues
on through her sons and grandsons.

ACKNOWLEDGEMENTS

I would like to thank everyone who has been a part of my eleven-month audacity code journey. Thank you, mom, for a lifetime of focused encouragement and support. Never once have you questioned my desires to build a life beyond the narrow limits of societal expectations. Thank you also for allowing me to rush through too many of our nightly dinners as I pecked out this tome on the computer.

Thank you to my big sister, Thelma, for spending a lifetime attempting to protect me from the remnants of the harsh realities she faced as a young black female in the segregated South. Your dedication to the promotion of equality of opportunity for all citizens is commendable.

I also would like to thank all of my nieces and nephews—Nia, Gerard, Willie, Kirby, Lyelle, Cairo, Reese, Regan, Wendall, Winston, Wayland and Kendrick for your unconditional love and favor. Each of you are a shining star of promise that generations of our family hoped, sacrificed, and prayed for.

To my friends, confidants, and cheerleaders—Darlene, Ella, Deborah, Yvette, Glenda, Lori, Ernest, Emmett, Sababu, Brian, Major and Herb thank you for your never-ending encouragement and support. You are always there for me and my dreams. Also, much gratitude to my 9-5 A-Team: Darla, Eckert, Shona, Manny and Reo for daily doses of laughter, connection, and encouragement especially in all things technical. Additionally, I would like to recognize the members of the 9-5 alumni association, Leticia, Hopelin, Randy and Mike, for their continued thoughtfulness and comradery.

Please allow me to publicly thank Sadie Simms, Cheryl Hayes, and Keisha Hayes for picking up many of the neglected pieces of my life during the endless months of crafting *The Audacity Code*. You each have my eternal gratitude.

Equally as important I would like to salute the following selfless members of the Women's Prosperity Network who have fully demonstrated their belief in me and my love of sharing African-American history: Linda Allred, Ellen McDonald, Nancy Matthews, Trish Carr, Susan Weiner, and Gail Dixon.

Finally, I would like to single out special appreciation and bundles of audacity to Judee Light and C. Simone Rivers for manuscript editing, editorial assistance, and other gifts.

If I omitted anyone who assisted in breathing life into *The Audacity Code*, please charge any oversights to my head not my heart.

NOTE ON TERMINOLOGY

From the early years of the 18th century through the late 1960s, the term Negro was commonly used to identify Americans of African ancestry and heritage. Any references to this racial identifier are for historical accuracy only.

CONTENTS

INTRODUCTION

The word *Audacity* carries a negative rap. Usually an act is considered audacious when someone is offended by the behavior of another. Cries of "How dare you!" and "Stay in your place" come to mind. Generations of African-Americans lived during the racialized era of Jim Crow which sought to enforce an artificial status of inferiority and subjugation upon Blacks. If an African-American deviated from prescribed behaviors in their interactions with members of the larger community, the most common retort included some charge of *audacity*. When an African-American chose to greet a white woman in a manner considered inadequately submissive or looked a white man directly in the eye, the standard response to such actions ofttimes involved life-threatening accusations of boldfaced *audacity*. But there is a flip side to the negative connotations normally associated with this term. Audacity is the confidence to venture past the status quo. It is a sense of self that necessitates rising above societal limits. It is the fearlessness that motivates the act of *coloring in black outside the lines.*

Sadly, when most people think of audacious African-Americans, only a few Black luminaries hold widespread top-of-mind awareness. If asked, the average citizen may recite the names of civil rights icons Reverend Dr. Martin Luther King, Jr. and Rosa Parks, along with perhaps the names of anti-slavery activists Harriet Tubman and Sojourner Truth. Others might add the name of Barrack Hussain Obama, the 44th President of the United States of America. Regrettably this extremely illustrious yet small group of icons represents only a narrow slice of African-American achievement. Similar to other groups of Americans, the expanse and depth of contributions made by Blacks is wide-ranging and not limited to the spheres of public service and civic engagement. Despite the legal, educational, and economic limitations historically placed on Black Americans, thousands approached life with a positive audacity. Some were enslaved while others were freemen. Some possessed extraordinary natural talents while others benefited from academic training. Some unleashed their imaginations to achieve their dreams, while others oriented their lives toward adventure and discovery. All built legacies worthy of investigation and celebration. All have something to teach. At their core existed a great pride in both their heritage and culture. They did not desire special treatment and only asked for opportunities equal to those of their fellow citizens. Each dedicated themselves to high standards of achievement, regardless of circumstances, and looked to the future with expectation and optimism. Still, what sustained them as their goals were unfolding? I assert that they all employed various combinations of *The Audacity Code.*

At the heart of the Audacity Code is a commitment to realize one's life purpose regardless of conditions, obstacles, or hindrances. Each of us must either embrace the status quo of our existence or choose to throw off the cloaks of conformity in our quest for individual fulfillment. Inherent to this code are the fundamental values and guiding principles to which all personal actions are aligned. Investigation of the behavioral North Stars of many accomplished African-Americans reveal lives guided by such success principles as adaptability, integrity, and accountability. Each of the thirteen personalities and triumphant biographies presented in this collection represent a life steeped in virtues and values that might, at times, seem in short supply.

The life stories and accomplishments of bold and daring African-Americans, like the mostly forgotten individuals featured in the following pages, regrettably are unfamiliar to most people. What a shame, for there is much to learn from their lives and personal successes in spite of their equally personal struggles. Each of these rainmakers developed his or her own audacity code. Some employed large quantities of determination, courage, and faith. Others relied on dauntless perseverance and optimism as they engaged the worlds in which they lived. Each sacrificed much. Some enjoyed celebrity status, while others labored in relative obscurity. More importantly, they all experienced an inner freedom and enhanced sense of personhood as they made their mark on humanity.

It is my hope that this salute to these great women and men will not only provide factual knowledge of their triumphs, but also positively affect interracial understanding. Instead of grouping African-Americans into limiting boxes of uniformity, or worse yet, sets of negative stereotypes, it is desired that some consideration be found for the individuality of each African-American citizen. Perhaps these twelve lessons in audacious living will add to a greater awareness of the potential and universal humanity that lies within each of us. The truths these remarkable Americans teach are outside the lines of color and available to all.

After each chapter, there is a succinct examination of the dominant audacity principle and personality traits exhibited in the highlighted biography. A resource list of books, videos, podcasts, and related historical sites is provided as well. Also, a timeline that features significant national events and legal decisions which affected the lives of those profiled is included.

I am fortunate to have been born into a family that liberally filled my life's cup with endless stories of African-American merit and achievement. The generous oral transfer of their knowledge and wisdom encouraged me to live a life of splendid audacity. It is my sincere hope that you, too, may find rich inspiration and joy in these stories of African-American excellence.

1. CHECKMATE

Elizabeth "Mum Bett" Freeman Circa 1744–1829

When Bett arose from her bed of matted hay, she did not know that the day ahead would be the worst of her young life. By the end of the morning, the ever-present love of her mother and father would become only a memory. Enslaved from birth, Bett's owner, Master Hogeboom, even in death, directed and dictated every aspect of her existence—including the structure of her family.

Pieter Hogeboom of Claverack, New York, had been a prosperous Dutch merchant and father of ten. Upon the reading of his will in 1758, his children learned that they were to divide equally amongst themselves all his "negroes and negresses." Without any consideration of family ties, the teenage Bett was issued to Hogeboom's youngest child Annetje.

The wife of John Ashley and the mother of four children, Annetje lived in Sheffield, Massachusetts. Although Bett's grief-stricken parents pleaded and appealed for her not to be taken away, their cries for mercy were unheeded. The life Bett had known with her family was about to end.

As her heartbroken mother attempted to calm her scared and bewildered child, an irritated voice barked for Bett to find a place for herself on one of the wagons that was headed from Claverack to Sheffield. On the 25 or so mile trip to Massachusetts, Bett's only thoughts were of reunion with her parents. But just as the sun began to hide its face for the night, Bett found herself deposited at the back door of the Ashley mansion—too afraid to go in, and too afraid to run.

By all measures, The Ashley's were the wealthiest and most prominent citizens of Sheffield, Massachusetts. The family operated a massive farm that produced corn, rye, oats, flax, wheat, and tobacco. They also raised various types of livestock, and owned iron and potash works, along with carding, plaster, grist, and sawmills.

Put to work the evening of her arrival, Bett was assigned to carry water and fan flies from the dinner table. In the days to follow, if a floor was dirty, Bett swept it. If the silverware was dull, Bett polished it. Whatever needed to be done, Bett was either to help with or perform the task herself. Annetje, however, was never pleased with any of Bett's efforts. Known to take pleasure in finding fault with everything and everybody, most people considered Annetje a demanding mistress who was easily provoked, ill-tempered, and flat-out mean. In other words, a witch by another name.

Bett endured almost a decade of forced exile from her mother and father before she received permission to marry an enslaved man from a nearby farm. Their union produced a daughter—Lil Bett. Finally, Bett had an outlet for the love she could not share with her parents. Being a wife and mother gave her hope for the future—a future that would materialize from her keen capabilities to listen and reason. Though she never spent a day in school, nor learned how to read or write, her ability to ponder an issue and come to a sound conclusion would be her *gift* to herself, her family, and the world.

Not long after the birth of her daughter, Bett noticed the Ashley house was abuzz with talk of freedom, rights, and revolution. The people of Sheffield were upset about how Great Britain treated them, and the Ashley house was one of the places they gathered to complain about and talk over their concerns. When they talked, Bett listened.

In January 1773, when a self-appointed committee of Sheffield's foremost citizens, which included five slaveholders, one known pirate, and one suspected counterfeiter, met and drafted a document that spoke to their grievances with Britain, Bett listened.

The Sheffield Declaration, also known as the Sheffield Resolves, blasted what its authors felt was British tyranny against their rights to undisturbed enjoyment of their lives, liberty, and property. While she waited on these men, Bett listened and thought a lot about the freedoms to which they claimed all people were entitled.

A few years later Bett listened to and considered the discussions she heard about another document—The Declaration of Independence—which spoke to certain rights and freedoms all people are due. Her husband even joined the Continental Army and fought against the British for these rights, which he was promised would also be his when the colonies won their war with Britain. Though her husband was killed in the line of duty in pursuit of these illusive freedoms, Bett continued to listen and think.

Five years later, Bett was still listening and thinking when she heard a public reading of the new Constitution of Massachusetts:

All men are born free and equal, and have certain natural, essential, and unalienable rights; among which may be reckoned the right of enjoying and defending their lives and liberties; that of acquiring, possessing, and protecting property; in fine, that of seeking and obtaining their safety and happiness.

Bett mulled over these words. She thought about her parents who never were free. She thought of her daughter who was not free. She thought about her husband who had died in his quest to be free. She thought someone in her family should experience freedom, and that someone should be her.

No one is sure what moved Bett from thinking about freedom to actively seeking it. Some say it was the result of a scar received from a red-hot kitchen shovel, courtesy of an enraged Mistress Annetje. Others said she just made up her mind that, like her deceased husband, she was going to fight for her freedom. Regardless of the reason, after more than 20 or so years of listening and thinking, Bett made the leap from listener to doer. From thinker to actor.

During the fall of 1780, the first item of business on Bett's way to freedom was to seek legal assistance from Theodore Sedgwick, an attorney who, years before, served as clerk to the committee that produced the Sheffield Resolves. Bett explained to Attorney Sedgwick why she wanted him to sue her master, John Ashley, for her freedom, and upon what she based her request for freedom. Aside from the legal implications of this request, Sedgwick knew acceptance of this case would put him in conflict with his friend, neighbor, and professional colleague, John Ashley, who at this point served as a local judge. In the end, Sheffield made peace with any potential social or political conflicts he might face and accepted Bett as a client.

Immediately, Sedgwick set about laying the legal groundwork for his case. First, he enlisted Tapping Reeve, founder of the first law school in the United States, as co-counsel. Next, he asked Bett to find a male slave to join the case, since women had limited legal standings in the courts. Bett persuaded Brom, a slave owned by the son of John Ashley, to become a co-plaintiff.

Nearly seven months later in May 1781, John Ashley and his son each were served with a writ of replevin—a form of action taken for the recovery of unlawfully obtained property. The writ stated that Bett and Brom where being unlawfully detained and should be released. Both writs were ignored. John Ashley also let it be known that he would only release Bett upon receipt of a bond which assured her return to him if she lost her case. On June 5th, the local Sheriff presented John with a bond and second writ of replevin. He then escorted Bett and her daughter off the Ashley property. While Bett awaited her August 21st trial, she lived with Attorney Sheffield, his wife, and their three children—Eliza, Frances, and Theodore.

On the appointed day, in the Great Barrington courthouse, the defendants John Ashley, Sr. and John Ashley, Jr. were represented by noted attorneys David Noble of Massachusetts and John Canfield of Connecticut.

Noble and Canfield argued that the Brom-Bett suit should be dismissed on the basis that Brom and Bett were the legal servants of the Ashley families. Sedgwick and Reeve countered that, based on the Constitution of Massachusetts, Brom and Bett were not the property of either of the defendants, and as such, should be freed. It took the jury just one day to deliberate the case. Their verdict: Brom and Bett were indeed not the property of anyone but themselves. The jury also commanded the defendants to pay 30 shillings in damages and court costs of six pounds. The presiding judge pronounced Brom and Bett **FREE!**

Initially stunned with the results of the trial, John Ashley quickly recovered and asked Bett to return to his home as a paid servant. She graciously refused. In response, John Ashley appealed his case to the highest court of Massachusetts—The Supreme Judicial Court. Six weeks later, he withdrew his appeal.

To symbolize her new status as a free person, Bett changed her name to Elizabeth Freeman. For the next 46 years, Elizabeth worked for, and was associated with, the Sedgwick family. She helped rear and raise all seven of the ten Sedgwick children who survived infancy. Bett also served as a community midwife and nurse.

Following 22 years of paid employment, Elizabeth bought a 19-acre farm on which she lived out her days with her daughter, grandchildren, and great-grandchildren. Never again would Elizabeth Freeman be separated from the ones she loved–her family.

###

"Any time while I was a slave, if one minute's freedom had been offered to me, and I had been told that I must die at the end of that minute, I would have taken it just to stand one minute on God's earth a free woman."

Elizabeth Freeman

Legally emancipated mid-wife and herbalist

Elizabeth "Mum Bet" Freeman

Image courtesy of Massachusetts Historical Society, Boston.

Elizabeth "Mum Bett" Freeman
Audacity Principle: Desire

The simple and profound idea that "Mum Bett" could muster an ounce of optimism and hopefulness for a life of freedom is almost unimaginable. To survive the everyday realities of being "owned" by another human being required "Mum Bett" and others of her station to live a   life of constant debasement, submission, and contrived inferiority. Elizabeth had lived through a forced and near lifelong separation from her parents, the death of her husband in the American Revolution, and decades of relentless abuse from Annetje Ashley for perceived infractions of insubordination.   Still "Mum Bett" continually tapped into her own inner sense of personhood to dare perceive, think about, and ponder life as a free human being—even if her freedom would have lasted just one minute. Not only was Mum Bett expectant about her and her daughter's future, she expressed her optimism and desires to someone in a position to turn her hopefulness into a winning legal argument.

After the Sheffield Sheriff failed on his first attempt to remove Bett from the Ashley household, Bett remained optimistic. She did not beg the Ashley's for forgiveness or pretend ignorance of the Sheriff's request. When the Sheriff returned the second time, to collect her and her daughter, Bett was ready to walk into her new life. Bett's desire was not for a decent life in the hereafter, but for a meaningful life while she was still on earth. Bett knew if she wanted a new life, she had to seek a new way.

What amazing things would you like to see happen in your life? Right now, not tomorrow, is the time to move your life forward.

Once Bett made the decision to legally fight for her freedom, she did not turn back. Surely, Mistress Annetje's wrath in the days and months leading to Mum Bett's departure from the Ashley household had not subsided or abated. Still, Bett put forth a courageous spirit and displayed epic emotional control as she awaited the day when she would hopefully leave the Ashley house one final time.

It is amazing what we can do when we let go of fear and choose a decisive plan of action, even if we do not instantaneously achieve our desired outcome.

The next hurdle between Bett and her desires involved asking for help. In relationship to the legal fight she planned to wage, Bett was aware of society's limited view of her as an uneducated and enslaved female. But Bett did not let what she did not have stop her from obtaining what she desired. Like the concepts of freedom that she had pondered over the years, Bett actively assessed and evaluated all the people who had come in and out of the Ashley home as it related to their ability and willingness to assist in her quest for freedom.

Finally, she settled on someone who possessed the right education and legal connections—Attorney Theodore Sedgwick. Bett did not let Sedgwick's friendship with the Ashley family stand in her way. Once she committed to a better life for herself and decided that she would act on her commitment, the next step was to march into Sedgwick's office and make her case. But her need for assistance did not stop there. Women had limited legal standing in Massachusetts, and Attorney Sedgwick advised Bett to seek a male co-plaintiff. Instead of losing heart, Bett readjusted and set out to persuade Brom who was owned by Colonel John and Annetje Ashley's son, Major General John Ashley, to join her case. We do not know what objections Brom may have presented, but he did make the choice to cast his lot with Bett's. Interestingly, after the Massachusetts Court of Common Pleas ruled in Brom and Bett's favor, Brom halfheartedly started a new life. As opposed to striking out on his own, he chose to work as an employee for his former master, Major General John Ashley.

Never let pride or fear stop you from seeking out others who can help you achieve your goals and desires. Having a request denied is not the worst thing that can happen. A denial is only confirmation that the wrong person was asked for assistance. Go back and think about what you really want, and the correct connection will manifest. When the pupil is ready, the teacher will appear.

"There is no easy walk to freedom anywhere, and many of us will have to pass through the valley of the shadow of death again and again before we reach the mountaintop of our desires."

Nelson Mandela

Former President of South Africa and Anti-Apartheid Revolutionary

Elizabeth "Mum Bett" Freeman Resources

BOOKS
Mother of Freedom (Mum Bett and The Roots of Abolition)
Ben Z. Rose
(Enfield Publishing and Distribution Company, 2009)

Grade Levels 3-5:
A Free Woman on God's Earth" The True Story of Elizabeth "Mumbet" Freeman, The Slave Who Won Her Freedom
Jana Laiz
(Crow Flies Press, 2009)

Grade Levels 4-6:
Mumbet: The Story of Elizabeth Freeman
Harold W. Felton
(Dodd, Mead & Company, 1970)

Grade Levels 7-9:
Mumbet: The Life and Times of Elizabeth Freeman: The True Story of a Slave Who Won Her Freedom
Mary Wilds
(Avisson Press Inc., 1999)

ONLINE SITES
blackpast.org
elizabethfreemancenter.org
mumbet.com
newenglandhistoricalsociety.com
massmoments.org

YOU TUBE VIDEO
Moments in Black History: Elizabeth Freeman

SITES AND MEMORIALS TO VISIT
Elizabeth "Mum Bett" Freeman Burial Site
Stockbridge Cemetery
Stockbridge, MA

The Colonel John Ashley House
117 Cooperhill Road
Sheffield, MA 01257

2. GOLD

Norbert Rillieux
1806–1894

Norbert missed New Orleans. He missed his younger brother Edmond and the hours they once spent in the woods which surrounded their father Vincent's plantation. His mother, Constance, a free woman of color, prepared the best meals Norbert had ever tasted. He wished he could see the beaming smile that flashed across her face whenever he asked for a second helping of just about everything she cooked. Sometimes he wished he could talk with someone who spoke Louisiana French. The way his family talked did not quite sound like the French he heard in class or on the streets of Paris, but Norbert knew that he was luckier than most. As the oldest of his parents' seven children, he understood that few others received the opportunity to pursue advanced education. He was grateful his father had arranged for him to study at the prestigious L'Ecole Centrale Paris where his natural curiosity and scientific abilities were challenged and enhanced. While other students struggled with the concepts and applications of physics and engineering, Norbert excelled.

As he neared the completion of his upper-level courses, Norbert happily prepared to return to New Orleans. But before he shipped out, L'Ecole Centrale Paris invited him to join the faculty as an Instructor of Applied Mechanics. When Norbert accepted the offer, he became the youngest teacher the renowned school had ever hired.

In addition to teaching, Norbert authored papers on the use of steam (water vapor) in industry. The leading scientific journals of the day contained numerous articles on new methods of production that utilized machines to create goods which traditionally were crafted by hand. This period, which would become known as The Industrial Revolution, was in full swing during Norbert's time in Paris. Of particular interest to Norbert were advances in the refining of sugar—the white gold from which many people in Louisiana made their living.

When Norbert was a boy, the English inventor Edward Charles Howard developed a fuel-efficient method of refining sugar. The Howard Method used steam to boil sugarcane juices in a closed kettle from which some of the air had been removed—a partial vacuum. Since the closed kettle reduced pressure, less fuel was needed to bring the sugar to a boil. The partial vacuum also reduced the amount of sugar lost to caramelization. This innovation advanced sugar processing, but Norbert felt that more efficient, less costly, and safer ways of sugar production were yet to be discovered. This opinion was backed by first-hand knowledge. His childhood memories of the frantic efforts that went into the processing of cane into sugar were as clear as polished glass.

For optimal quality, the juice housed inside the cane stalks required processing within 48 hours of harvest. To meet this two-day timeline, enslaved workers worked around the clock grinding newly picked rods of cane into sugar. Haste, along with semi-primitive processing methods, on average, cost the life of one enslaved worker per two thousand tons of refined sugar. Many more lost limbs as they fed ten to twelve-foot rods of cane into the roller mills used to squeeze the sweet liquid from the mashed stalks.

Norbert correctly recalled how workers involved in the first steps of sugar production, shoved fresh cane into a long tube connected to mule-powered cylinders that crushed the stalks and released their naturally sweet juice. As the juice was collected, it was directed into a sweltering hut, where it underwent continual boiling in a cascade of four copper kettles of decreasing size. The manual transfer of the molten juice from kettle to kettle, known as *The Jamaican Train,* was performed using long-handled ladles. The workers also were responsible for the removal of any impurities or waste that bubbled up to the top of the hot liquid. When the juice was spooned into the last kettle, it was allowed to cool and harden into a brick of brown sugar. The slightest incorrect movement or placement of a ladle at any point in *The Jamaican Train* could result in painful and disfiguring burns and scars.

Aside from the human costs involved in sugar processing, enormous amounts of wood were required as fuel. Since wood is a one-and-done resource, any increase in sugar yields required an almost equal increase in logging. Managing the roaring flames that energized the boiling process was still another dangerous aspect of production. Similar to lightning striking a combustible object, sparks from the fires that heated the cane kettles could morph into an inferno within the span of two to three minutes. Indeed, turning sugarcane into sweet salt was a high-risk business. But for successful planters, it produced handsome profits.

Norbert's writings on the use of steam in sugar production were not challenged, but he could not find a French sugar producer willing to finance and test out his theories. However, his writing did stir interest in New Orleans.

Edmond Jean Forstall, a Louisiana sugar baron and president of the soon-to-be-built New Orleans Sugar Refinery, had a problem. A number of his customers were not satisfied with their sugar orders. The quality was uneven and unreliable. If he did not find a solution to this problem, rival growers in the Caribbean Islands and South America stood ready to serve his clients. Forstall thought maybe New Orleans' native son Norbert Rillieux and his ideas about the expanded use of steam in sugar production might solve his quality issues. Perhaps Norbert could be enticed to return home.

Forstall's offer of the Chief Engineer's job at the New Orleans Sugar Refinery was excitedly accepted by Norbert. Returning home and being afforded a platform from which he could test out his sugar production ideas and theories was a dream come true.

Soon after his arrival in New Orleans, a bitter dispute erupted that pitted Norbert's new boss Edmond Forstall against Norbert's father and younger brother, also named Edmond. Apparently, Mr. Rillieux and his son, Edmond were one of the contracting companies building the refinery for Forstall, and the three men clashed over the construction of the new sugar refinery. Acting on his strong sense of family loyalty, Norbert resigned from his newly acquired job. An enraged Forstall vowed to exact revenge on the Rillieux clan!

Although he no longer had a laboratory on which to try out his ideas, Norbert continued to develop his concepts. Within the year, he built his first sugar processor for Zenon Ramon, another local sugar planter. As with many inventions, Norbert's first prototype was faulty and quickly scrapped. As he worked to refine his ideas, he also dabbled in real estate, but lost all the money he made during the financial crisis known as The Panic of 1837.

Although his attention was no longer divided between real estate and inventing, it still took another four years for Norbert's ideas about automating sugar production to materialize into a working model. And it took an additional two more years to secure a manufacturer capable of mass-producing his invention. Altogether it took nine long years for Norbert to perfect his designs of how best to use steam in the production of sugar. After all the false starts, disappointments, and late nights spent perfecting his sugar boiler, finally in 1843, Norbert was awarded United States patent number 3,237.

Technically, Norbert's creation was a multiple-effect evaporator but was more commonly known as the "Rillieux sugar boiler." Unlike the Howard Method of boiling sugar cane juices in a partial vacuum, Norbert's invention created a complete vacuum, which encased all the containers utilized in turning cane juice into sugar. The vacuum reduced the amount of air around the containers, which in turn lowered the temperature and amount of fuel needed to bring the cane juice to a boil. Specifically, steam from the first vat was released and transferred to a second receptacle, while steam from the second container was released to heat the third cauldron. The fourth and final vat was heated by steam from the third boiler. Norbert's vacuum also eliminated the manual transfer of cane juice or syrup from one container to another. As a result of this mechanization, the quality of the sugar produced was standardized. Burnt and discolored sugar was no longer a problem. Each subsequent batch matched the first batch in color, taste, and quality.

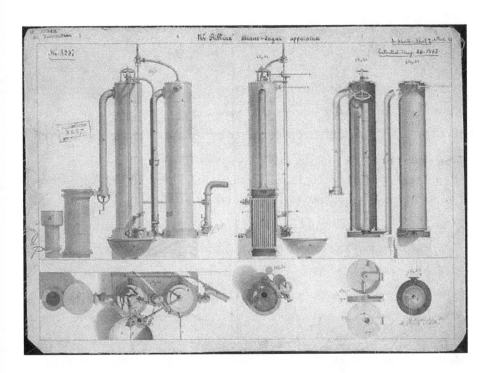

Norbert Rillieux Steam Sugar Apparatus Patent Drawing
Image Courtesy of Special Media Services Division of the National Archives and Records Administration.

Norbert's evaporator was produced in three sizes. The smallest refined 6,000 pounds of sugar per day. The medium-sized boiler doubled daily output to 12,000 pounds of sweet goodness, while the maximum daily capacity of the largest processor was 9 tons. Due to the massive increases in daily output, the Rillieux multiple-effect evaporator paid for itself within a year.

But Norbert was not quite done. He charged a rental fee to plantation owners who bought his sugar boiler. The amount of the fee was a percentage of the savings in labor and fuel costs a planter would realize from using the Rillieux boiler. To determine the rental fee, Norbert would run a 24-hour test of his machine on the buyer's land to determine the amount of fuel and labor used by his boiler along with the amount of sugar it produced. He would compare the test data against the plantation's historical fuel, labor, and sugar production records. Part of the savings achieved with the Rillieux boiler were rebated back to Norbert in the form of a rental payment. For both sugar producers and Norbert, the multiple-effect evaporator was a sweet deal indeed!

Norbert's evaporator also did not cause injury, required only one worker to operate, and the sugar it produced tasted the same batch after batch. Most importantly, it drastically reduced the cost of processing sugar. What could possibly go wrong?

An employee of Merrick and Towne, the Philadelphia, Pennsylvania, firm that manufactured Norbert's evaporator, stole the design drawings and set up shop in Magdeburg, Germany. The rogue employee was able to produce the multiple-effect evaporator but lacked knowledge of how to properly install the machine. Without proper installation, the counterfeit machines were basically worthless piles of metal. These bogus machines harmed Norbert's reputation in Europe. But on the North American side of the Atlantic Ocean, word of Norbert's phenomenal processor spread, and orders from Mexico, Cuba, and the Virgin Islands poured in. Norbert and his machine were popular, but his social status in New Orleans was declining. As a mixed-race person, Norbert was treated only marginally better than an enslaved worker. His first attempt to secure a patent for his invention was rejected due to assumptions the patent examiner made about his racial classification. As America inched closer to civil war, Norbert no longer was allowed to travel from one place to another without a pass written by a white person granting him permission to do so. Not possessing a pass could result in arrest or imprisonment.

Norbert had multiple innovative ideas, but the rejection of a mosquito abatement plan he developed to prevent the frequent outbreak of yellow fever in New Orleans may have been the last insult that soured Norbert against his birthplace. Norbert's plan would have drained the swamps that surrounded the Crescent City and improved its sewer system. These two actions would have greatly reduced the size of the breeding grounds in which the disease-carrying pest flourished. The number one opponent of his plan was Edward Forstall—his one-time employer and later Rillieux family nemesis.

Deeply unhappy with life in New Orleans, Norbert returned to Paris and immersed himself in the study of Egyptology and the decoding of Egyptian hieroglyphics. Over time, he returned his attention back to sugar production and received another French patent for producing refined sugar from sugar beets using their own vapors.

For enslaved workers, the Rillieux sugar boiler was a double-edged innovation. While the processing of sugar became less treacherous and grueling, its increased profitability led to the planting of more sugar cane. More acreage under cultivation called for more enslaved laborers for tilling, planting, and harvesting.

Today the concepts Norbert used in his sugar processor are the standard by which all industrial evaporation is benchmarked. His multiple-effect evaporation process under vacuum is used in the production of glue, soap, condensed milk, and other consumer products. Items once considered luxuries are now enjoyed by the average person. What a sweet legacy.

"The skin of yesterday's sugarcane is a harvest to an ant."
Swahili Proverb

Norbert Rillieux
Audacity Principle: Commitment

Most young professors in the infancy of their career would have been satisfied to have their writings published in popular scientific journals. But not Norbert Rillieux. He wanted more. He was certain that he could improve upon the process used to refine sugar from sugar beets. However, he was unsuccessful in his search for a French planter who would be willing to sponsor his research.

When the opportunity to return to New Orleans as Chief Engineer of a sugarcane refinery presented itself to Rillieux, he excitedly set sail for home. Of course, he did not know that his father and new employer would soon engage in a disagreement so intense that he would feel compelled to resign from his near-perfect job. In a matter of months, Rillieux went from being a highly regarded professor to an unemployed dreamer.

After a period of time, a local sugarcane grower agreed to finance Rillieux's sugar-processing theories into a workable invention. Rillieux's best efforts produced a failure. His next two tries did not pan out either. It took almost a decade of mistakes, do-overs, and fresh starts to see his vision materialize. Still Rillieux kept the faith. He did not wait for the best circumstances to appear, nor did he let mistakes end his experimentation.

When you attempt to avoid mistakes and failures, seldom will you discover anything new about yourself, others, or life. Mistakes are proof that you are trying, creating, and exploring. Many have been conditioned to think that mistakes are a negative reflection of their efforts or abilities. But in reality, mistakes demonstrate that you are doing something right, while commitment allows you to keep moving forward even when sidetracked. When all is well, commitment is effortless. It is only when you slosh through the storm, like the postal workers who live by the creed *"Neither snow nor rain nor heat nor gloom of night stays these couriers from the swift completion of their appointed rounds,"* that you began to realize the extent of your commitment.

Like Rillieux, you do not need to wait for perfect life circumstances to commit to your dreams. Circumstances are never completely ideal, and you miss out on a lot of life waiting for just the right moments. When going after what you want from life, do not delay the journey waiting for the best time to get started. Make a commitment to wholeheartedly give your all to the tasks at hand and stay the course until you are triumphant. What fruits of your labor would appear if you exhibited commitment similar to that displayed by one of America's most gifted sons?

One of the underlying themes of Rillieux's life was his devotion to sugar processing. Even after he moved back to France and devoted himself to the study of Egyptian hieroglyphics, Rillieux still worked to find a fuel-efficient process for the extraction of sugar from sugar beets. As he entered the sunset years of his life, a 75-year-old Rillieux finally realized the results of improving the extraction of sugar from beets that he had so long ago set out to achieve. As a young professor, Rillieux probably did not believe it would take nearly 50 years for his interest in sugar beets to bear fruit. Most likely, only when he looked over the arc of his life, did he see that it took nearly half a century to realize his initial goal.

The French naturalist Georges-Louis Leclerc, Comte de Buffon, reportedly said *genius is only a greater aptitude for patience.* Clearly Rillieux's long-term devotion to the lowly sugar beet is an excellent example of Leclerc's sentiment. Like Rillieux, *you* have the capacity to harness the willpower needed for the long haul. Surely life will offer roadblocks and detours, but do not let delays, interruptions, or lethargy erode your commitment to the work at hand. If you find yourself off-track, tap into your storehouse of memories as to why you began your journey in the first place. You may even have to relaunch your efforts. But, if you have already left the starting line, why not finish the race?

"To make our way, we must have firm resolve, persistence, tenacity. We must gear ourselves to work hard all the way. We can never let up."

Ralph Bunche
African-American Nobel Peace Prize Laureate

Norbert Rillieux Resources

BOOK
Reaching for Freedom: Paul Cuffe, Norbert Rillieux, Ira Aldridge, James McCune Smith
David Harbison
(Scholastic Book Services, 1972)

ONLINE SITE
usslave.Blogspot.com

YOU TUBE VIDEO
Londie Smith Channel: Norbert Rillieux

SITES AND MEMORIALS TO VISIT
National Historic Chemical Landmark
Dillard University
2601 Gentilly Boulevard
New Orleans, LA 70122

Bronze Bust
Louisiana State Museum
Cabildo
701 Chartres Street
New Orleans, LA 70116

Burial Site:
Père Lachaise Cemetery
16 Rue du Repos
Paris, IdF 75020
France

3. MASTER

Ira Frederick Aldridge
July 24, 1807–August 7, 1867

ACT I

Ira pondered what he could say to his father that would make him understand. He knew that his father only wanted the best for him, but preaching the gospel was not his calling. Yes, he loved words and the power they carried, but turning sinners into saints was not for him. He wanted to melt the hearts of men another way—from the stage, not the pulpit. No, Ira could not name one colored man who made his living as an actor, but he had been bitten by the acting bug and was determined to find relief.

It is not that Ira was not appreciative of the sacrifices his father, a street vendor and minister, had made on his behalf, it was just that he didn't want to preach the Gospel. He had always been thankful to have been born to parents who were free. He was not someone's property or workhorse. Ira was even more thankful that he lived in New York City where he could go to school and expand his mind and outlook.

As a student at the African Free School No.2, which was charged with preparing its students to live as free people in a free country, Ira Frederick Aldridge received an education equal to that of many whites. The African Free School was operated by and reflected the philosophies of the New York Manumission Society, whose members included men of eminence and distinction such as Alexander Hamilton and John Jay, two of America's founding fathers. It was here that Ira was first bitten by the acting bug. As the leading man in Romeo and Juliet, Ira's flair for the dramatic was on full display.

To the dismay of his father, Ira nursed his acting fever by frequent trips to the white-owned upper-class Park and the Black-owned African Grove theatres. Both offered large servings of Shakespearian drama. At the Park, Ira was a spectator restricted to the Blacks-only gallery. At the African Grove, he was a participant. That is, until he was arrested in mid-performance.

Apparently, the management of the Park and other white-owned theatres viewed the African Grove as a competitive and cultural threat. Grove customers were routinely harassed by the police for behavior that was deemed acceptable at white-owned theaters. Even its actors were not immune from harassment. In the middle of a production, hired thugs rushed the stage and beat Ira and other Grove actors. The beating was followed by arrests. The battered actors were only released from custody after they promised not to perform any more Shakespeare. Blacks performing the works of the most celebrated English language playwright was equality gone too far.

Ira's arrest further hardened his father's attitude against the theatre. Why would Ira choose a path that brought shame and disgrace to their family name? How did Ira expect to make a living as an actor? Why would he throw away his God-given gifts? It was then that Ira, to his father's dismay, decided to launch out on a journey that would change his life.

ACT II

Ira did not believe his luck. He and the popular British actor and producer, James Wallack, were passengers on the same ship headed to Liverpool, England. Wallack was sailing back home. Ira was starting a new life.

Without any real opportunities to work as an actor in America, Ira thought maybe he could break into the English theatre scene. Unable to afford a ticket, he signed on as a ship steward for passage, but had no solid prospects for work once the ship docked. However, by the time their ship sailed into port, Wallack had hired Ira as his personal valet and agreed to introduce Ira to his theatre contacts.

Now with a job and place to live, Ira turned to the work of reinventing himself. First, he decided to change his personal story. As opposed to being known as the son of a preacher, he decided to assume the persona of a Senegalese Fulani prince. In time, promoters would refer to Ira as the African Tragedian. As his star power increased, he became known as the African Roscius, indicating a level of dramatic excellence equal to that of renowned Roman actor Quintus Roscius Gallus. Ira understood the power of branding. He, not others, would control his image.

Within a short period, Ira was cast as Othello, the lead character in a widely popular Shakespearian play by the same name. Othello tells the story of a Black general in the Venetian Army who is tricked by Iago, one of his officers, into believing that his wife is an adulteress. In the heat of passion, Othello murders his wife. Upon discovering his officer's deceit, Othello kills himself. Normally a white actor in blackface played the role of Othello. Ira's portrayal would be the first time a Black actor was cast in the role. Not bad for a 17-year-old.

A few months later Ira was cast as the lead actor in *The Revolt of Surinam* or *A Slaves Revenge*. The main character Oroonoko is an African prince. How fitting this character mirrored Ira's new persona!

In between acting gigs, Ira managed a theatre in Coventry, England, and worked to perfect his portrayals of other high-profile Shakespearian characters such as Macbeth, Richard III, and Hamlet. He also began to hone his comic chops as Mungo, a dim-witted, West Indian butler, who would sing and dance on cue from the play *The Padlock*.

It took Ira eight years to make it to London's mainstage and his welcome was uneven. When asked to fill in for well-known actor Edmund Kean, Ira's portrayal of Othello was loved by the audience who showed their approval through thunderous applause and the waving of hats. Many of the critics were more concerned with his skin color and his gall to play a Black character. Probably the harshest criticism came from the *Figaro* newspaper: "Force him from the stage... and force him to find [work] in the capacity of footman or street-sweeper, that level for which his colour appears to have rendered him peculiarly qualified." A day later, the production closed.

A deeply disappointed but undefeated Ira, returned to plying his craft in the English countryside and provinces of Ireland, Scotland, and Wales.

For nearly twenty years he performed in small towns, villages, and hamlets. Audiences loved him and other actors sang his praises.

Act III

Ira's time had come. Confident in his abilities as a performer and producer, a middle-aged Ira set out to conquer all of Europe. No longer would he confine himself to England and her territories.

Wherever Ira toured he was a sensation. Cologne, Frankfurt, Leipzig, Vienna, Berlin, Prague, Budapest, Serbia, Russia, Switzerland. Audiences adored him, and critics raved about his craftsmanship. While he performed in English, local actors translated his words into their native tongue. But it was not the words that won audiences over. It was Ira's masterful use of body language. He voiced the most subtle to the most profound emotions through his tone of voice, facial expressions, and body movements. When he expressed breathtaking regret, the audience could feel his anguish. When he spoke of heart-stopping despair, the audience felt the tears in his voice.

Ira was acclaimed by both the common man and the exalted. In Russia, working class theatre goers celebrated Ira by storming his carriage and bodily carrying him from the theater to his hotel. They also made him the highest paid actor in the country as they gobbled up tickets to his shows. Royal leaders like Friedrich-Wilhelm IV, the King of Prussia, awarded Ira the Prussian Gold Medal for Art and Sciences. The Emperor of Austria presented him with the Medal of Ferdinand, and the Duchess of Saxe-Coburg-Gotha bestowed a knighthood on him. Ira also received the Maltese Cross from Switzerland and the Golden Cross of Leopold from Russia. In other words, he was THE BOSS.

Of course, all the London theatres *now* wanted a piece of the action. Ira politely acknowledged London's new-found love of all things Ira by performing a few shows in London now and then. However, Ira no longer needed London's hard-won approval and continued to spend most of his time outside of Britain.

After years of crisscrossing Europe, Ira turned his attention to America. As the hometown kid who made it big, Ira wanted to go home, even if only for a brief time. Ira had always been a strong abolitionist. He publicly spoke out against the horrors of slavery and donated large sums of money to anti-slavery organizations. Often on the last night of an engagement, Ira shared with the audience his desires to see the abolishment of slavery. Given that the American Civil War was over, and all Blacks were freedmen, Ira felt that the time was right to return to the United States.

Ira thought he would tour America the same way he had toured England. He would perform in both large and small cities. Everyone would have an opportunity to experience his art. The plans for his stateside tour called for 100 performances. But it was not to be.

While on tour in Lodz, Poland, Ira suddenly took ill and died. He was buried two days after his death in the city's Evangelical Cemetery. When word of his unexpected death spread, no doubt there were many who did not want to believe Sir Ira Frederick Aldridge had taken his final curtain call.

Sixty-five years later Ira and his innate theatrical abilities were memorialized in Shakespeare's hometown of Stratford-upon-Avon, England. At the town's Shakespeare Memorial Theatre, Ira and his artistry were saluted with the placement of his name on one of 32 memorial chairs dedicated to Shakespearian masters.

"The guy who takes a chance, who walks the line between the known and the unknown, who is unafraid of failure, will succeed."

Gordon Parks

African-American documentary photojournalist

Ira Aldridge- Circa 1852- From a daguerreotype by William Paine of Islington. Printed by The London Printing and Publishing Company. Public domain via Library of Congress and Wikimedia Commons

Ira Frederick Aldridge
Audacity Principle: Fearlessness

Very few parents encourage their children to pursue acting as a career. The prospect of sporadic employment, financial instability, and fickle audiences are the hard realities most adults spout to their budding drama kings and queens. During the early 1800s when Ira was a boy, acting was not a respectable profession. Theatres were rowdy venues where behavior more akin to that displayed at football games was the norm, and the style of acting was more minstrel than masterful. But for Ira, the bite left by the acting bug demanded a cure.

Ira risked all the societal advantages at his disposal to feed his passion for the theatre. He willingly gave up highly desired opportunities available only to a free person of color in a slave-oriented society, mainly a seminary education and the respect that would be bestowed upon him as a member of the clergy.

Instead he hitched his hopes of fulfillment to the writings of Shakespeare and Aphra Behn, the world's first professional female playwright. Ira questioned why only white actors dressed in blackface should be allowed to play Black characters. Why couldn't he dress in white face and play roles written for white actors? He also rightly understood that significant rewards require significant risk.

Ira's initial interactions with the theatre were bittersweet. He relished breathing life into a character; however, he was equally as disheartened by the New York theatre scene and its racial animosity when he was arrested on stage while in mid-performance. The charge—disturbance of the peace for providing Black theatre goers a choice in where to spend their leisure time, and more importantly, their money.

Unlike many people who are safety experts when it comes to risk, Ira accepted that he did not have a shot at achieving his dreams if he played it safe. He chose to be all in, not lukewarm, when it came to the manifestation of his passions and desires.

Your life is like a seed in a barn. In that, if allowed to take risks outside of the barn, you will find unforeseen opportunities to succeed. Of course, you can choose to live and die in the warmth of the barn as a seed, or you can maximize your potential when you choose to leave the barn and start a new life under layers of wet, soggy dirt. But as soon as you become comfortable with earth's environment, you have to break through layers of soil and mud in search of an audience with freedom and vitality from the sun. And still you face peril—as it is only a matter of time before you are plucked up and tossed into a pan of boiling water. From there you most likely will travel to a farmer's dinner plate where you will bring pleasure and nourishment to a hungry family. Most people probably would like to leave a noble legacy, but are you willing to put everything on the line to fulfill your destiny?

When Ira crossed the Atlantic to ply his gift of acting, as expected, some critics found the mere thought of a Black actor repulsive, while others applauded his early portrayals of well-known Shakespearean characters. After nine years of perfecting his skills in community theaters, Ira received a much-desired invitation to perform in London at the fashionable Covent Garden. Following his second performance, the Covent rolled up its welcome mat and sealed its doors to the Black Roscius. Naysayers cited his inexperience; pessimists blamed his race; doubters decried his performance. As for Ira, he kept moving forward in his quest to find his personal best.

Ira did not just act. He created his own opportunities for artistic and financial success, all while honing a completely new style of acting. He ditched the exaggerated gestures and stage presence, popular with leading actors of his day, for a more natural and realistic interpretation of emotions and feelings. His authentic and subtle interpretations of man's primal instincts—fear, revenge, and greed—advanced the craft of acting and satisfied audiences' appetites for heart-stopping entertainment.

With a wife and child to support, Ira could not afford the luxury of being unemployed. He took his shows to the hamlets, villages, and small towns scattered across England, Scotland, Ireland, and Wales. Sometimes he made great money, earning half of all profits his performances generated. Other times he barely covered expenses. Regardless of his financial state, Ira continued to trade comfort and conformity for risk and the possibility of great reward.

When the time came for this black butterfly to spread his wings across Europe, Ira was ready. In four separate European tours, Ira cast his spell over both royalty and commoners. All gladly filled the coffers of local theater owners for the opportunity to be transported to a place of wonder which only Ira could deliver.

It took 25 years of diligent and hard work for Ira to taste the ripe fruits of his labor. Before he was an instant success, he plied and refined his abilities throughout the bush and byways. Sometimes he played before packed houses, other times he entertained rows of empty seats. Sometimes he was paid handsomely, other times he was cheated out of his wages. Sometimes his worst effort was celebrated, other times his best labor was rejected. Each time Ira mounted the stage, he emptied his reservoir of talent. Nightly he faced potential failure as he exposed himself to the real possibilities of rejection, judgment, and criticism.

Though silenced by death at the age of 60, Ira continues to serve as a model of what is possible for those unafraid to leave their cocoon.

Similar to Ira's experiences, your road to personal fulfillment may be peppered with false paths, landmines, and booby traps. It also might be studded with golden opportunities, lucky breaks, and divine intervention. Reward tends to find those who strip off all unnecessary layers of safety gear in their quest to experience the best of life's possibilities.

"Challenge your fears! Find your potential."

Bishop T.D. Jakes
American Bishop, Author and Filmmaker

Ira Frederick Aldridge Resources

BOOKS
Ira Aldridge: Celebrated 19th Century Actor
Martin Hoyles
[Hansib Publishing (Caribbean) Limited; UK ed. Edition, 2008]

Grade Levels: 2-3
Ira's Shakespeare Dream
Glenda Armand
(Lee & Low Books, Inc., 2015)

ONLINE SITES
100greatblackbritons.com
bbc.co.uk
chesapeakeshakespeare.com
famousbiographies.org
historyextra.com
mentalfloss.com
medium.com

SITES AND MEMORIALS TO VISIT
Blue Plaque Historical Marker
5 Hamlet Road
Upper Norwood
London SE19 2AP
Borough of Bromley

Bust
The Theatre Royal, Drury Lane
Covent Garden
London, England

Bronze Plaque
Royal Shakespeare Theatre
Stratford-upon-Avon, England

Burial Site:
Evangelical Cemetery Augsburg
Lodz, Poland

C.R. Patterson and Sons Company, 1873–1939

Charles Richard Patterson, 1833–1910
Frederick Douglas Patterson, 1871–1932

Charles Richard Patterson was born in Virginia, but he did not speak much about his life there. Since his late teens, Charles, better known as C. R., had lived in the village of Greenfield, Ohio, a stop along the Underground Railroad. This railroad was a web of secret routes and safe houses used by Blacks to escape slavery before the American Civil War. When C. R. entered manhood, like his father and two of his eight brothers, he made his living as a master blacksmith. Early on, C. R. was employed by Dines and Simpson Coach and Carriage Company. In time he was promoted to shop foreman and supervised several of his former white co-workers in the building of horse-drawn carriages.

By most standards during this time, C. R. settled down and started his family late. He was in his early thirties when he and Josephine Outz were married on the 4th of July. Their union produced five children—two boys and three girls. Tragically, their second daughter, Nellie, died before her fifth birthday. In addition to building his family, C. R. served as a church trustee and Sunday School teacher at the Greenfield African Methodist Episcopal Church. He also held office in Cedar Grove Lodge Number 17, Free and Accepted Masons.

As his family and community standing grew, C. R. desired to open his own business. However, instead of entering the market as a sole proprietor,

C. R. partnered with J. P. Lowe to build and sell carriages. During the height of the Patterson-Lowe 20-year partnership, the firm employed between 10 and 15 craftsmen and produced 28 different types of horse drawn vehicles, which ranged in price from $120–$150. At that time only 45% of the country's population earned more than the annual poverty income of $500. Clearly Patterson and Lowe's clientele were members of the middle and upper class. After two successful decades of a mutually beneficial relationship, C. R. bought Lowe's share of the business and re-branded the operation, C. R. Patterson & Sons.

C. R. and Josephine named their first son after the noted abolitionist Frederick Douglass. More inclined toward academics than his brother Samuel, Frederick was valedictorian of his high school and was a popular student-athlete at The Ohio State University. In addition to sports, Frederick also served as Business Manager and Editor of the Personal and Local sections of the student newspaper *The Lantern*. Samuel, the couple's youngest son, joined his father in business, but after a short illness, he died at the age of 24. Determined to pass the business down to the next generation, a grief-stricken C. R. asked Frederick to give up his teaching career and return home.

Whatever technical shortfalls Frederick may have possessed were overshadowed by his astute marketing and operational skills. Frederick did not view the family business as carriage making, but rather he saw the larger picture and viewed C. R. Patterson & Sons as a provider of transportation which included manufacturing, repairs, and service. As an extra bonus, Frederick was an easygoing salesperson who possessed exceptional verbal and promotional writing skills.

Three years after joining his father in business, Frederick noted the first signs of change that would define C. R. Patterson & Sons legacy. That year there was one "horseless carriage" or automobile per 65,000 citizens. Seven years later, which was the year before his father died, the ratio of cars per person was one per 800 residents. Obviously, traveling by horse and carriage would soon become a thing of the past.

With a young family of his own and fully installed as head of C. R. Patterson & Sons, Frederick set about building upon the business foundation his father had created for the Patterson clan. While Frederick worked to move C. R. Patterson & Sons into the automotive age, the company still had a healthy custom carriage business. Known as a relentless promoter and advertiser of the firm's products and services, Frederick continually improved upon the outfit's stellar customer service. He produced an annual 100-page catalogue, published a monthly newsletter, and featured customer testimonials in advertisements. Frederick also coined the company's tag line—*If it's a Patterson, it's a good one.*

Operationally, his fingerprint was on the company's two-year carriage warranty. This forward thinking also extended care to customers bringing in carriages for repair, as they were insured against shop damages. Repair customers were also provided with loaner buggies. When business was sluggish, Frederick offered at-cost pricing and credit terms for qualified buyers. Skeptical or new customers were eagerly invited to tour the company's facilities and inspect its raw materials. Outside of Ohio, Frederick made the rounds to important trade shows and conferences in his relentless battle to stay ahead of competitors. He was even quoted in a New York Times article.

Always a good writer, Frederick applied his love of words and the dramatic to product ads and press releases. A sample of his promotional writing ability is on full display in this advertising snippet on what it takes to maintain a good business:

> *"The real test comes in holding good patronage. Personality won't do it; cheap goods, even low prices, won't do it, and a whole lot of talk won't do it. What is the secret? Simple indeed but must be persistently pursued. Give honest value, give dependable quality, go to your patrons personally with every assurance that their interests are always safe-guarded."*

When not shoring up the carriage business, Frederick worked toward the production of an automobile that could represent the company's future.

In 1915 when Frederick premiered the Patterson-Greenfield automobile, you could count on one hand the number of Blacks employed in the automotive industry. At America's largest car manufacturer—Ford Motor Company—only two Blacks were on the payroll. A few more may have owned cars, but no other Blacks had produced a viable automobile.

A fully equipped Patterson-Greenfield could comfortably seat five passengers and cost $650, about $100 more than a Ford Model T. And unlike Henry Ford who produced his millionth car the same year C. R. Patterson & Sons produced its first, the long-term prospects for the production and sale of the Patterson-Greenfield automobile were uncertain. Still, Frederick emptied his verbal arsenal in promoting Patterson's most ambitious creation. Frederick described the Patterson car in *The Greenfield Republican* newspaper as:

> *In my judgement there isn't a machine on the market that sells at or less than $1000 that will equal the Patterson-Greenfield. Our car is made with three distinct purposes in mind. First - It is not intended for a large car. It is designed in size to take the place originally held by the family surrey. It is not intended as an omnibus or carry-all. It is a 5-passenger vehicle, ample and luxurious. Second - It is intended to meet the requirements of that class of user, who though perfectly able to spend twice the amount, yet feels that a machine should not engross a disproportionate share of expenditure, and especially it should not do so to the exclusion of proper provisions for home and home comfort, and the travel and varied other pleasurable and beneficial entertainment. It is a sensibly priced car. Third - It is intended to carry with it (and it does so to perfection) every convenience and every luxury known to car manufacturers. There is absolutely nothing cheap about it; nothing shoddy. Nothing skimpy and stingy. Delicate and finished in its appointments and when compared to other cars costing twice the price, the chief difference lies in the size, and yet, to the average man, the smaller size is to be preferred.*

A true count of the number of automobiles produced by C. R. Patterson & Sons varies from 30 to 150. During the same three-year period that the Patterson-Greenfield was manufactured, the daily output for Detroit-based manufacturers was no less than 1,800 automobiles per day. To remain viable, the Patterson company would have to compete on volume, not craftsman-ship. Without access to institutional capital markets, the future of the Green-field-Patterson was a black hole sucking resources out of more profitable areas of the company. Some may see Frederick's decision to halt production of the Greenfield-Patterson as a failure, but Frederick saw the demise of the Patter-son-Greenfield as an opening into a more profitable market—school buses. However, before C. R. Patterson & Sons transitioned into the field of student transportation, it capitalized on its automobile production knowledge and built a lucrative auto repair and aftermarket accessory business. From electrical repairs to production and installation of closed cover tops onto Model T cars, C. R. Patterson and Sons was able to once again do what it did best—meet the needs of its customers.

Two years after the final bolt was tightened on the last Patterson-Greenfield, Frederick incorporated the Greenfield Bus Body Company with a capital stock of $50,000. Frederick's keen sense of analyzing market trends served him well in this new venture. As the country was moving away from the one-room school-house to consolidated school districts that drew students from large geographic areas, the transport of students to and from school required new transportation options. Unlike their entry into the automobile industry, where C. R. Patterson & Sons manufactured the entire car, Frederick chose only to produce school bus bodies that could be affixed to a chassis manufactured by another firm.

C. R. Patterson & Sons' reputation for excellent workmanship and rela-tionships with customers across Ohio and the larger region of Kentucky and West Virginia facilitated its profitable entry into the school bus market. After its first ten years of manufacturing bus bodies, Patterson & Sons' bus products were used in 36% of Ohio's urban and 15% of its rural districts.

School bus built by C.R. Patterson and Sons Company
Image courtesy of Greenfield Public Library, Greenfield, Ohio.

Business was so good at the beginning of the Great Depression that C. R. Patterson & Sons was forced to operate around-the-clock shifts in order to meet demand.

Like his father before him, Frederick brought his two sons into the business. Frederick P. Patterson, a mechanical engineer, designed the company's bus and other commercial bodies such as overnight campers and moving vans. His brother Postell Patterson's strengths lay in hands-on operations. Unfortunately, due to Frederick's unexpected death at age 61, they were thrust into leadership roles at probably the most perilous time of the company's existence.

Following closely behind their father's death, changes in school bus safety standards required bus bodies to be made of steel. C. R. Patterson & Sons' bodies were crafted from wood. The new standards weakened or destroyed both large and small manufacturers. The Great Depression was in full force and access to capital the firm needed to move from wood to steel bus bodies was difficult to acquire. Both Frederick P. and Postell valiantly worked to keep the firm afloat. They took out second and third mortgages on properties the firm had routinely mortgaged to manage cash flow shortfalls. Because of the firm's excellent credit history, local banks and suppliers either lent the business more money or relaxed payment terms. Still the company's financial woes deepened and the property from which C. R. Patterson & Sons conducted business was under threat of a sheriff's auction. In desperation, the brothers placed their hope for financial salvation in an offer from the Gallipolis, Ohio Chamber of Commerce. If the Patterson grandsons, Frederick P. and Postell, would relocate the business to Gallipolis, they could have free use of a building in exchange for jobs for some of the town's unemployed citizens. Reluctantly, Frederick P. and Postell relocated their families and operations to Gallipolis.

Though the company operated as The Gallia Body Company, it could not outrun its problems. New orders continued their downward spiral as school districts were forced to trim expenses. The ability to buy needed equipment was hampered due to the firm's poor credit rating. Even the training of new employees proved problematic as some workers struggled with learning the skills needed to put the company back on its feet. Even though they managed to build a few bus bodies from steel, the number of orders they secured were not enough to return the business to financial health. C. R. Patterson & Sons had run out of lifelines. One by one, both family members and relocated employees returned to Greenfield. Only Postell and his wife Kathleen were present to lock the doors one last time on the 74-year-old family business.

Still the people of Greenfield, Ohio, remember C. R. Patterson & Sons with an enduring sense of pride.

###

"The wise man banks on straight methods, honest hard labor and grit to hold out to the end. He is a fool who depends on tricks and sharp practices, at the best his success will be short lived, and his self-contempt long lived."

Frederick Douglas Patterson
The Greenfield Republican

C. R. Patterson & Sons
Audacity Principle: Integrity

C. R. Patterson possessed first-class blacksmith skills. He had ambitious hopes for his future and knew the social fabric of the day required he be twice as good as his competitors to achieve even half of their success. But C. R. possessed a no-fail audacity trait that gave him a lifelong competitive edge—sterling integrity. He demonstrated integrity in every area of his life through words, deeds, and actions. When the average Black was considered a resource, whose labor was for the enrichment of others, C. R. Patterson held the position of foreman responsible for an all-white crew of blacksmiths. Clearly more than technical skill helped him obtain such an unusual and rare position for a Black man. When the Village of Greenfield denied his son admittance to the only local high school on the basis of his race, C. R. challenged the decision. When diplomacy did not work, he took his son's case to the courts, where he won.

It is easy to have integrity in the absence of conflict, discord, or dissention. It is the sign of true integrity to refuse to compromise your principles when others stand to accuse you of being ungrateful, unreliable, or untrustworthy. But integrity requires us to act according to the principles, beliefs, and values we claim to hold—even when no one else is looking.

Integrity was the cornerstone of all of C. R.'s business activities. Without inherited wealth to finance inventory or to provide cash during off-seasons, C. R. purchased parcels of land that he would mortgage in order to provide needed cash flow to pay business expenses. Regardless of business or personal conditions, C. R. met his loan obligations and promises to his customers. When his son Frederick took over management of the firm, he was able to finance the firm's entry into car manufacturing, in part due to his father's established credibility.

Imagine a Black man in 1915 being able to finance the manufacturing of not one, but dozens of automobiles for sale to the general public. Although Frederick entered the automotive industry too late in the game to sustain profitability, he took the lessons learned and used them to become a dominant player in the Ohio school bus market. In some areas, Patterson buses represented up to a third of all school buses on the roads. Without government mandates, Patterson continued to improve on bus safety and rider comfort. Customers came to know that the Patterson tag line "*If it's a Patterson, it's a good one*" was backed up by truth in action—integrity.

Can you say the same about your reputation? If family members, neighbors, co-workers, or business associates were asked to think of a phrase that captured your essence, could they comfortably say you are "a good one?" Do others have reason not to think of you as a reliable wing person, a trustworthy associate or consistent ally? Do you play hide and seek with the truth or cut corners when you think no one is paying attention?

Unfortunately, after Frederick's sudden death, his young sons, Frederick P. and Postell, were thrust into the business at the worst time. Construction requirements for school buses were changing from wood to all metal, while the Great Depression had a suffocating stranglehold on business investments. At first, they practiced what they had seen their father do to generate cash flow. But when sales of their products did not produce enough income to meet the company's loan obligations, the younger Patterson men traded on their grandfather's and father's good names and placed second mortgages on a number of the company's real estate holdings. Unable to make payments on the firm's outstanding debt, Frederick's sons accepted an invitation to relocate the bus company from Greenfield to Gallipolis, Ohio. Neither Gallipolis nor the brothers were able to hold up their ends of a bargain crafted in desperation. Surrounded by the carnage from their business dealings in both Greenfield and Gallipolis, and their reputations in tatters, the third generation of Patterson entrepreneurs finally closed the business.

Imagine the sting of betrayal felt by the firm's long-term bankers and financial backers. It was one thing to not pay a mortgage note due to the effects of the Great Depression, but another to find out that the same piece of property they had lent money against carried another mortgage of which they knew nothing.

Relationships, which are at the heart of all personal and professional inter-actions, are built and survive on trust. It is imperative that you hold yourself accountable for the commitments you make. You must show up, especially when it is not comfortable. Keeping your word and delivering on the promises you made is the only way to gain the lasting confidence of others. For it is far better to go down in honor than in disgrace.

"The slow man with integrity will ultimately catch the swift one who has none."

Unknown

C. R. Patterson & Sons Additional Resources

BOOK
The C. R. Patterson and Sons Company: Black Pioneers in the Vehicle Building Business, 1865-1939
Christopher Nelson
(Create Space Independent Publishing Platform, 2010)

ONLINE SITE
https://magazine.northeast.aaa.com/daily/life/cars-trucks/cr-patterson-and-sons

YOU TUBE VIDEO
History in Motion: Patterson-Greenfield Automobile Company (First Black Owned Automobile Company)

SITES AND MEMORIALS TO VISIT
Greenfield Historical Society
103 South McArthur Way
Greenfield, OH 45123

Burial Site:
Greenfield Cemetery
750 N. Washington Street
Greenfield, OH 45123

5. SPUDS

Junius George Groves
April 12, 1859–August 17, 1925

Junius Groves had reached the "Promise Land." Like the Old Testament Israelites who fled Egypt, thousands of Blacks in 1879 left the American South, with its widespread racial violence and limited economic opportunity, for a new life in Kansas. Known as Exodusters, many dreamed of a brighter future as homesteaders. Junius did not just dream of a bright future in a land of milk and honey, he skillfully set about working to bring forth his vision of a *remarkable reality*.

Without much formal education and only 90 cents in his pocket, the first thing the former Kentuckian needed to do was find a job. Junius learned that he could hire on at one of Kansas City's meat packing houses. He quickly realized why. Aside from the work being dirty and unsanitary, it was also extremely dangerous. Not satisfied with his lot, Junius restarted his job search for work he knew and loved, tilling the soil or farming.

Due to the tremendous number of Black laborers in search of work, farm wages were depressed. Like others, Junius needed to survive and accepted a job in nearby Edwardsville, Kansas, for a paltry 40 cents a day. Instead of complaining about his pitiful wage or only putting out 40 cents worth of effort, Junius did the opposite. Within three to four months' time, he was promoted to foreman which paid almost twice as much. A lot of folk would have been satisfied with this arrangement, but not Junius.

In search of still greener pastures, Junius quit his "good job" and restarted his search for suitable employment. Finding nothing to his liking, he returned to Edwardsville where Jake Williamson, his former employer, suggested he consider becoming a sharecropper. As a tenant farmer, Junius obligated himself to give a third of anything he produced to Williamson in exchange for the use of nine acres of land, a team of mules, a few tools, and enough seed to bring in a decent crop. Junius accepted the deal and planted three acres each of Irish potatoes, sweet potatoes, and watermelons. With his first plantings in the ground, Junius then made the most significant decision of his life. He asked Matilda E. Stewart to marry him, even though he did not have enough money of his own to pay for their marriage license.

The day after they wed, Matilda joined Junius in the field as co-owner of Junius' vision of a *remarkable reality*. When Junius and Matilda brought in their first harvest and settled their debts, the newlyweds showed a profit of $125. Instead of celebrating their success with perhaps a new dress or some perfume for Matilda, the couple invested every dollar they earned into their vision for a *remarkable reality*. They spent $25 on a cow, another $25 on seed, and the remaining $50 on a lot in Kansas City. They also increased the number of acres they farmed from nine to twenty. Again, after all the debts from their second year of farming were paid, the couple showed a modest profit. This time around they invested their earnings into a team of mules.

In the third year of their marriage, Junius and Matilda rented a 66-acre farm and subleased a portion of the land to another tenant. They also raised pigs and other animals and sold milk and butter. During the winter they sold firewood. All their efforts led to a $2,000 bank account. Accustomed now to wagering everything for their *remarkable reality*, Junius and Matilda emptied their account and bought an 80-acre farm. Unable to purchase the farm outright, the couple accepted a $1,400 balloon mortgage that required final payment in a year. If the Groves were not able to meet the terms of the agreement, they would lose all rights to the farm and the $2,200 they had paid toward its purchase.

The community naysayers immediately predicted defeat for the couple. No way could they meet the demands of their mortgage. Something would go wrong. The weather would work against them; their return would be too small. There was not any way Junius and Matilda could work that size farm.

The negative talk began to weigh on Junius—maybe he and his wife had taken on more than they could handle. Maybe the result of all their efforts up until this point would end up wasted if they could not meet this milestone in their vision for a *remarkable reality*.

However, when Junius began to question the authority on which the naysayers stood, he found quicksand. Not one of them owned or showed promise of owning anything. They had already given up on their dreams, if they ever had them. Or maybe they had tried and failed. Maybe they could not find the courage to go the distance. Whatever the case, Junius knew he had to cut their doomsday prophecies out of his mind, the way he cut the weeds away from his young seedlings. With renewed determination and the force of a Kansas dust storm, Junius and Matilda went into overdrive. Not only did they knock the air out of their balloon mortgage, they ended the year with money to spare. And as before, they put their surplus to work for their long-term *remarkable reality*.

During the next nine years, both Junius' and Matilda's family and farming operations continued to grow. Their household was a lively place, with a brood consisting of almost a stair-step gang of eleven. As the family grew, so did their agricultural holdings. After they paid cash for two nearby farms, Junius and Matilda acquired two additional homesteads, which increased their total holdings to 500 acres. Long gone were the days of three acres of white potatoes and three acres of sweet potatoes. In addition to growing various types of potatoes, Junius and Matilda brought in freight car loads of seed potatoes, which they sold to other farmers. In their fruit orchards, the pair cultivated thousands of peach, pear, apple, and cherry trees. They also maintained grape and apricot orchards. Like their farm, Junius and Matilda's *remarkable reality* was no longer a someday vision, but a fast-evolving reality.

With so much acreage under their control, Junius and Matilda were able to construct a self-supporting and self-contained estate. In addition to a massive two-story barn, the couple operated a granary and warehouse and owned the latest models of potato planters, weeders, and diggers. By the turn of the 20th century, the family lived in a 14-room home that sported gas lighting, telephone service, and indoor plumbing in each bedroom. They also built a roller rink on their property for the enjoyment of their children and their playmates. In the span of roughly a dozen years, the Groves family progressed from a one-room shack and two mules to an expansive, manicured estate. But Junius and Matilda were just getting started.

The year the Groves celebrated 25 years of marriage Junius was anointed "The Negro Potato King." In all actuality he was "The Potato King of the World." In 1905 the Groves' farming operations produced more than 720,000 bushels of potatoes, nearly 121,500 bushels more than any other grower in the world. Even though Junius had a limited education, he viewed science and technology as a farmer's best business partners and allies. He eagerly implemented the knowledge his sons learned at Kansas Agricultural College. The Groves' potato yields were so bountiful that, at the height of the picking season, as many as 50 laborers, both black and white, worked to bring in the crop.

In addition to growing their own tubers, Junius and Matilda also bought and sold potatoes grown by neighboring farms. They raised, bought, or shipped out so many potatoes that the Union Pacific railroad built a dedicated spur or secondary track to their farm from its main line in Edwardsville, Kansas. In addition to interstate sales, the Groves' potatoes were shipped to Canada and Mexico. With the profits from their various agricultural activities, the Groves operated a general merchandise store and invested in bank stocks and international mining operations. They also financed both their sons' and their daughters' college educations.

Determined to do as much good as they could for the public, Junius and Matilda provided much needed affordable housing through their development of the Groves Center. The showpiece of the community was a golf course built for the enjoyment of their guests and local Black residents.

Matilda and Junius Groves

Image courtesy Kansas State Historical Society

Not everyone was happy with Junius and Matilda's success. The most unnerving display of jealousy and envy was the mysterious fire that destroyed the family's 14-room home. Though a bit shaken, Junius and Matilda replaced it with a brick 20-room mansion. Even the best shot of a cowardly arsonist could not stop the unfolding progress of Junius and Matilda's vision.

How sad it would have been if Junius and Matilda had given up on their dreams or allowed the calls of the pessimists to take root in their minds. Instead they drowned out the choir of naysayers and their siren songs of failure, gloom, and despair. Fortunately for them and many others, Junius and Matilda did not give up on their dreams, and the shadow of their *remarkable reality* still lingers as a reminder of the power of a vision.

"I have begun everything with the idea that I could succeed, and I never had much patience with the multitudes of people who are always ready to explain why one cannot succeed."

Booker T. Washington
Founder of Tuskegee Institute

Junius George Groves
Audacity Principle: Vision

Junius knew what he wanted. He desired to live a Christian life, provide for his family, and uplift his community. These were almost impossible yearnings for the average Black man living in the American South during the late 1870s. With the end of Reconstruction, which had provided some means of advancement for African-Americans, Black males of working age became the objects of widespread discriminatory labor practices. These lopsided and unfair arrangements were reinforced by so-called Black laws that attempted to control Black labor and any upward mobility such labor might provide.

Key to this labor grab was convict leasing schemes. These arrangements between law enforcement agencies and the politically connected centered upon the arrest and imprisonment of large numbers of Blacks on flimflam or trumped up charges of vagrancy. As pawns in this unholy alliance between government and private enterprise, those arrested were leased out to work for free as repayment to society for their supposedly criminal behavior. In other words, slavery 2.0. Under these types of circumstances, anyone can see why a man of Junius Groves' character would walk hundreds of miles to re-establish his life in the Midwest.

But mere relocation did not satisfy Junius. He owned and trusted the vision of how he wanted to live his life and committed himself to the achievement of his goals. At first, only he cared for and nurtured his vision. Then he met Matilda. She, like Junius, existed on next to nothing in the way of material goods. However, she too, possessed the ability to envision and foresee a *remarkable reality*, the likes of which few blacks and many whites dared deem possible. Aside from their romantic compatibility, Junius and Matilda were each other's steadfast support and vision keepers. Imagine what their lives would have been like if their commitment to a *remarkable reality* did not sync.

Holding on to the visions and dreams of youth is hard even for those whose lives were substantially better than that of the Groves. Now imagine holding fast to that vision, through the birth of 14 children and the early deaths of two. Imagine holding on through the dizzying weather conditions of the Midwest—floods, droughts, tornadoes, blizzards, and scorching summer heat. Or living with your visions through life in a dilapidated run-down shack as you worked the land six days a week, from sunup to sundown.

Imagine three straight years of pouring every dime you could spare into building your vision—no family outings that required the expenditure of money, no store-bought toys for your children, no weekly appointments with the barber or hair stylist, even when you deserved it.

This is the reality Junius and Matilda lived during the lean years of their vision. Only once did Junius flirt with doubt, but he quickly vanquished it from his thoughts. During the darkest of times, the Groves persevered, even when it took every bit of their mental energy to flip the coin of fear on its head to refocus their thinking on its reassuring side—faith.

Bringing a vision to life requires discipline and the ability to stay focused. Discipline to stay the course when it is just you in the cheering section. Discipline to forgo short-term gratification for long-term gain. Discipline to go through all the birthing pains required to bring your vision to life.

Junius and Matilda's vision was not only about financial gain and recognition. Their vision gave their lives a sense of purpose and direction. They saw themselves as up-lifters of their neighbors and community. They found great joy in service. They provided jobs, housing, and recreational opportunities for all who would avail themselves of these resources. A stingy, self-centered vision tends not to bear fruit and shrivels up like a prune.

What are you too afraid to dream possible? What is your vision? Who could you inspire through the realization of your life's task? Perhaps once others see your vision materialize into a *remarkable reality*, they also might trade in their daydreams and begin their own journey to possibilities.

> *"Dreams can become a reality when we possess a vision that is characterized by the willingness to work hard, a desire for excellence, and a belief in our right and our responsibility to be equal members of society."*
>
> Janet Jackson
> Pop Icon and American Singer, Actress, and Songwriter

Junius George Groves Resources

BOOKS
The Booker T. Washington Papers, Volume 7: 1903-1904
Louis R. Harmon and Raymond W. Smock, Editors
(University of Illinois Press, 1977)

Grade Levels: Preschool-3rd
No Small Potatoes: Junius G. Groves and His Kingdom in Kansas
Tonya Bolden
(Knopf Books for Young Readers, 2018)

ONLINE SITES
blackpast.org
kshs.org

YOU TUBE VIDEO
Junius G. Groves: From Slave to Wealthy Potato King

SITE TO VISIT
Bruce R. Watkins Heritage Center
Hall of Fame
3700 Blue Parkway
Kansas City, MO 64130

6. ELEGANCE

Isaac Burns Murphy
1861–1896

Isaac Burns Murphy began life a few weeks after the start of the American Civil War. He was the only child of formerly enslaved America Murphy and Jerry (Skillman) Burns. Like many other young Black men, Jerry decided to fight for his family's freedom, and served as a private in Company C of the Kentucky based 114th Regiment of the Union's Colored Infantry.

Unfortunately, three and a half months after Confederate General Robert E. Lee surrendered his troops at Appomattox Court House, Jerry Burns died. Per his military file, the cause of death was unknown. There is a high probability that Jerry died from either war injuries, or from one of the rampant communicable diseases, like typhus, which plagued the military and civilian residents of Kentucky's Camp Nelson.

Following the death of her husband, America and young Isaac moved to Lexington, Kentucky. Beginning afresh, America chose to live by the mantra of newly freed Blacks—*"Let Labor and Education be Your Motto."* She found work as a domestic and encouraged Isaac in his studies at one of the five schools designated for children of the recently emancipated.

Determined to become a homeowner, America scrimped and saved whatever money she could. In 1870, after five years, she bought a plot of land, making her one of only a few African-American women in Lexington who owned real estate. Her dream, however, soured four years later in 1874 when the Freedman's Saving and Trust Company commonly known as the Freedman's Bank collapsed. America, along with an estimated 65,000 other Black depositors lost their life's savings due to the bank's implosion. While America mourned the loss of her financial future, she received a life altering diagnosis of tuberculosis. In the late 19th century tuberculosis, like many other infectious diseases, equaled a near certain death.

Upon learning of her illness, America's immediate response was concern for Isaac's future. She did not want him to live the life of a destitute orphan. After she weighed her limited options, America chose to approach James T. Williams, owner of the first horse to win the Kentucky Derby, regarding Isaac becoming a horse exerciser at his stable. At this time, the majority of the trainers, grooms, jockeys, and exercise riders were African-American. Thirteen of the 15 jockeys who raced in the first Kentucky Derby were Black.

Isaac may not have known how his future would unfold, but he did know that this opportunity required him to trade in his mother's constant encouragement and schoolbooks for life in a barn. Along with the other exercise boys and the stately animals he would grow to love, Isaac lived and slept in the Williams' stable. Schoolwork now involved the provision of water and feed to his horse playmates. Homework entailed the removal of waste and the distribution of new straw and wood shavings to each animal's stall. Occasionally Isaac massaged the horse's muscles and brushed their hair. He also had the responsibility of reporting any physical or emotional changes in the stock to Eli Jordan.

The first horse Isaac received permission to mount was aptly named Volcano. In a predictable eruption, the volatile Volcano immediately threw the inexperienced Isaac to the ground. Understandably Isaac's pride took a hit, but the ever eager would-be-jockey refused to let Volcano have the last word. He lifted himself from the ground and again climbed onto Volcano's back for the second of many lessons in the science of riding. Similar to an artist, Isaac needed to learn not only the technical aspects of riding, but every detail about any horse to which he might be assigned. Specific details such as the animal's disposition and personality under pressure, its morning mood, its afternoon attitude, and its behavior around other horses.

Isaac loved his new life and started a jockey apprenticeship in less than two years. Fortunately, his debut race on Lady Greenfield proved not to be an indicator of what was to come. Not only did he lose his first race, he came in dead last.

Between the moral teachings of his mother, and that of Eli Jordan, Isaac's fellow jockeys considered him a professional outlier. He did not smoke, gamble, or cheat in races. Contrary to popular belief, Isaac only passed liquor across his lips for medicinal purposes or on special occasions. A number of his rivals considered him to be a goody-two-shoes. Another sign of the budding phenom's sense of respectfulness and family occurred when he took his grandfather's last name-Murphy. The exact reason for this reverential gesture remains unknown, but more than likely America was happy her boy would keep alive her father's surname.

When Isaac's mentor Eli Jordan relocated to Frankford, Kentucky to work for the well-regarded Hunt-Reynolds' Fleetwood Stables, Isaac soon followed. It was during this period of his career that Isaac established a reputation as a consistent winner and man of character, even though his tenure at Fleetwood started off rocky.

The incident which led to four months of anxiety for Isaac and Hunt-Reynolds occurred at the Queen City races held in Cincinnati, Ohio. While Isaac worked his way toward the finish line, a rogue rider deliberately cut in front of Isaac and his horse, Classmate, bringing the steed temporarily to her knees. The offender then darted in front of another rider, Link Gross. Unlike Isaac, Link retaliated by using his whip to slash the wrong doer across the face. With all three horses literally bottled up against each other, blood from the offender's face wound splattered onto Isaac's shirt. For whatever reason, the offender blamed Isaac not Link for his facial injury. Isaac received the un-merited punishment of one-year suspension and a fine of $25, the equivalent of about $500 in current purchasing power. Following this incident, Hunt-Reynolds released Isaac from his contract, leaving the defenseless and innocent rider without any viable means of making a living. After an investigation into the event, the president of the Queen City races, Edgar Johnson, apologized to Isaac for his incorrect and consequential actions against the neophyte. This negative hit to Isaac's professionalism also caused him to lose four months wages and four months of prime racing opportunities.

Subsequent to the Cincinnati incident, Isaac went on to win a number of leading races the next year—the Louisville Cup, the Tobacco Stakes, the Clark Stakes, the Tennessee Stakes, and the Merchant Stakes. On the other hand, his mother, America, continued to lose her battle with tuberculosis. In August of 1879 Isaac's mother reunited with her husband, Jerry Burns, in death. Thirteen months later Isaac's employer, J.W. Hunt- Reynolds, unexpectedly died while attending a family reunion in North Carolina.

The death of his mother and Hunt-Reynolds caused Isaac to pause and consider the state of his personal life. He somberly realized that he had no one with whom he could intimately share both his successes and failures. He rhetorically asked *will I always face the world alone*. Racing required him to constantly move from one event to another, hence he never stayed in one place any substantial length of time. Eventually, Isaac did find the woman of his dreams, Lucy Carr. From the beginning of their relationship Isaac and Lucy were inseparable. After their marriage, Lucy traveled to all of Isaac's races until his retirement. Together, they zig-zagged across the country from the Midwest to the East Coast and from the Upper South to the Far West.

In 1883 after his marriage to Lucy, Isaac made a bold decision about his career. He decided that only he, and no one else, would control his destiny. Instead of signing a contract which bound him to one stable, Isaac placed a newspaper advertisement in the *Kentucky Live Stock Record* which announced his availability to work as a contract rider. In less than a week, Isaac received so many offers for his services that he requested the newspaper cancel the ad. Of the offers he considered, Isaac finally negotiated a unique riding agreement with Ed Corrigan, an influential Canadian-born track owner and horse breeder.

Corrigan agreed to pay Isaac a $5,000 retainer to race Corrigan horses in premier events, while permitting Isaac the option to ride for different owners when he chose to do so. To secure Isaac's services, rival owners had to pay Isaac's monthly retainer fee of $25. Regardless for whom he was riding, Isaac required a minimum of $25 per win and $10 per loss along with flexible bonus payouts, depending on the race. This arrangement put Isaac in the same economic class with many doctors, lawyers, and politicians. During the 1886 racing season, California land speculator and millionaire, Elias J "Lucky" Baldwin, raised Isaac's yearly contract compensation from $6,000 to $10,000 in appreciation of the stellar success Isaac achieved while riding Baldwin horses.

At his peak, Isaac turned in win after win. He won his first Kentucky Derby riding Buchanan owned by William Cottrill. He also rode Ed Corrigan's Modesty to victory at the more prestigious American Derby held in Chicago, Illinois. The second and third year of his contract with Lucky Baldwin, Isaac won back-to-back American Derby's. Being a three-peat winner of the American Derby, Isaac's career catapulted from star to celebrity status.

In 1887 alone, Isaac's image appeared on at least three different tobacco cards, which were the equivalent of today's baseball, basketball, or football trading cards. In the following four years, Isaac won another American Derby and back-to-back Kentucky Derby's. He also was victorious in the first Great White Hope sporting face-off that carried loud tones of America's growing racial animosity toward Black athletes.

June 25, 1890 was the day, and Sheepshead Bay in Brooklyn, New York was the place to be. The anti-black faction of racing put their money on Jockey Ed "Snapper" Garrison and the highly heralded Tenny. Isaac saddled up California Gold Rush multimillionaire James Ben Ali Haggin's Salvator. Garrison lived up to his aggressive reputation as he lashed, pounded, and nearly whipped Tenny to death in his push to beat Isaac to the finish line. Isaac on the other hand, employed his signature cool and even-paced style to overtake Garrison and Tenny as he guided Salvator to the winner's circle.

Aside from bragging rights for some race enthusiasts, the negative economic fallout from this clash loomed large for others. A number of professional gamblers lost tens of thousands of dollars on the Garrison vs. Murphy race, and those on the unsavory side of racing decided they needed to deal with their number one problem —Isaac Burns Murphy. Their hatred of the

Issacs Burns Murphy celebrating his victory on Salvator at the home of Matt Byrnes.
Image courtesy of Keeneland Library Collection.

brown equestrian increased exponentially after widespread circulation of a photo featuring Isaac relaxing after his and Salvator's win over Garrison and Tenny. The image of Isaac enjoying his victory, as a social equal with whites, proved to be the proverbial last straw for the renowned rider's detractors. Less than a month after the publication of the supposedly offensive photo, Isaac's nemeses unleashed a sinister plot to bring down the "*uppity king of the track.*"

On August 26, 1890 at New Jersey's Monmouth Park, Isaac was poisoned, and his saddle tampered with in such a manner that he probably would have lost his seat, the race, and possibly his life. At the very least, he would have incurred serious injuries. However, within moments of taking his mount, Isaac pulled his horse Firezi to the rear of the pack and held on for dear life until all the other horses had passed him. When he did make it to the end, he let go of the reins and tumbled to the ground. To better understand how much this race had been considered a sure win for Isaac, the trainer Matt Byrnes, at whose home Isaac had celebrated his win over Garrison, lost $50k due to Isaac's inability to effectively compete.

Pending an examination of this bizarre event, Isaac received a 30-day suspension. Rumors and newspaper reports spoke of how bookmakers who had "inside knowledge of the race" walked away with thousands in winnings. The official, but secret, investigation of the event confirmed poisoning, not liquor, caused Isaac's physical troubles and subsequent loss of the race. None of the perpetrators were ever publicly identified or punished.

A year after winning the 1891 Kentucky Derby, the holders of Isaac's final riding contract, Ehret, McLewee, and Allen, terminated the agreement before the completion of the season. Although Isaac possessed a self-reported career win/lost ratio of 44%, his style of racing had become a relic of the past. In less than twenty-years, horse racing evolved from a sport of leisure for the genteel to a game of greed and winning at all costs. Sportsmanship and integrity became artifacts of bygone days. After Isaac pushed back against Ehret, McLewee, and Allen's attempt not to uphold their contractual obligations, the trio eventually paid Isaac's ten-thousand-dollar retainer, which was still due irrespective of their decision not to use his services.

To celebrate their tenth wedding anniversary in 1893, Isaac and Lucy hosted a lavish party at their Lexington mansion. They renewed their vows in front of guests who traveled from across the country for one of the social events of the year. Less than 24 months later, 35-year-old Isaac Burns Murphy completed his mother and father's broken family circle . Complications of the flu and the long-term effects of bulimia contributed to Isaac's early death. In order to make the assigned riding weight for many of his races, Isaac subjected his body to all sorts of quick weight loss practices. These schemes eventually took a harsh toll on his digestive and cardiovascular systems.

More than five hundred people passed through the Murphy home to express their condolences to Lucy and pay their last respects to the phenomenal jockey. Lucy Murphy laid her husband to rest in the style to which he had become accustomed, refined elegance. The diminutive Isaac lay in a replica of the copper casket use to hold the body of Civil War hero and United States President Ulysses S. Grant. After the funeral service, mourners followed the body to African Cemetery Number 2 where they said their final goodbyes.

That same spring, the Supreme Court in *Plessy v Ferguson* voted 7 to 1 to uphold the separation of the races in public facilities. This landmark judicial decision swung open the gates for the wholesale purge of Black jockeys from American racetracks. Henry King in 1921 became the last African-American to ride in the Kentucky Derby during the 20th century.

Isaac Burns Murphy never compromised his principles or integrity in order to be the best. Elected the first jockey inducted into the National Museum of Racing and Hall of Fame, nearly sixty years after his death, the *"King of the Track"* was receiving the honor and respect he so justly earned.

###

"I ride to win."

Isaac Burns Murphy
Three-time Winner of Kentucky Derby

Isaac Burns Murphy
Audacity Principle: Accountability

When Isaac Murphy began his career as a jockey, the sport of horse racing represented the idealized masculine virtues of honor and chivalry esteemed by 19th century American gentry. As this leisurely pastime grew more commercial and involved outlays of money larger than friendly wagers, the integrity of many racing enthusiasts began to fray.

Countless riders accepted bribes, conspired to fix races, and exhibited other forms of cheating which eventually moved the state legislatures of California and New York to ban betting on horses during the early years of the 20th century. Riders capitulated to fast money and pledged their allegiance not to fans, but to easy payoffs. Isaac Burns Murphy did none of this, and through a self-instilled sense of accountability, rose to the pinnacle of propriety and success.

Integral to Isaac's accountability was a sense of ownership for his actions. From the smallest task to the most consequential races, Isaac did not afford himself the luxuries of finger pointing, excuses, or blame. His singular aim was to win and win correctly. From the continual development of his physical, tactical, and mental abilities, Isaac increased the level of faith others placed in him and he in himself. He proved one race at a time that the quality of his work merited trust and confidence. Failures required remediation and successes required analysis. All required accountability.

Off-the-track, Isaac's accountability to his wife and marriage are worth noting. Instead of leaving Lucy in Kentucky to oversee their home and other properties, both Isaac and Mrs. Murphy traveled together to all his races. Everyone likes a winner, and some fans go to extreme measures to insert themselves into the lives of the celebrated. Who would mind if Isaac drank to excess, cheated on his wife, or spent the night gambling away his earnings? Clearly Isaac did. When he signed up for a race, his wife signed up as well. His dedication to Lucy equaled his dedication to racing. He respected and honored both of his loves with almost equal passion. All which lead to the question, what takeaways related to accountability might be gleaned from how Isaac conducted his affairs?

In both the professional and personal arenas of his life, Isaac employed three fundamental tenets of accountability:

1. Discipline to do the work required. This usually involved sacrifice and delayed gratification versus an attitude of one and done.
2. Demonstration of dependability and reliability. Isaac meant what he said and delivered what he promised. He performed a task the 15th time better than he performed it the 10th time.
3. Dedication to the job, not the show. Isaac did not just sell the sizzle; he sold the steak as well. Follow through is more important than elaborate promises or inconsistent performances. Isaac aimed to become a sure bet, not a one hit wonder.

Are you a champion in these areas of performance? Which parts of your life could use an accountability tune-up? Follow Isaac's lead of finding value in ownership of your efforts.

Isaac Burns Murphy Resources

BOOKS
The Prince of Jockeys: The Life of Isaac Burns Murphy
Pellom McDaniels III
University Press of Kentucky; Illustrated Edition (October 22, 2013).

Grade Level: 2-3
Perfect Timing: How Isaac Murphy Became one of the World's Greatest Jockeys
Patsi B. Trollinger
Benjamin Press (February 1, 2011)

Website
BlackPast.org

YOU TUBE VIDEO
Prince of Jockeys: The Life of Isaac Burns Murphy

SITES AND MEMORIALS TO VISIT
The Isaac Murphy Memorial Art Garden and Historic Marker
577 East 3rd Street
Lexington, KY 40508

Burial Site:
Kentucky Horse Park
4089 Iron Works Parkway
Lexington, KY 40511

Matthew Alexander Henson
August 8, 1866–March 9, 1955

No one knows for sure when Matthew Henson first heard the call of the wild. Maybe it was the tales and stories of an old seafarer, "Baltimore Jack," that stirred his imagination and desire to explore the world for himself. What is known is that, at age 13, Henson walked the 40 miles from Washington, D.C., to the wharfs of Baltimore, Maryland, to answer this call.

Province would lead Henson to an unusual old skipper, Captain Childs, who took pity on the orphaned teen and honored his request to work as a cabin boy on the *Katie Hines*. Not only did Childs provide an opportunity for Henson to become a citizen of the world, he poured a lifetime of knowledge into his young charge. For two hours each day, Childs helped Henson better his reading and writing. He also taught the pre-teen history, geography, and navigation. For five years, Henson soaked in the beauty and culture of such far-flung ports of call as China, Russia, the Caribbean, and North Africa. But when Captain Childs died, Henson no longer had the guidance or protection of his mentor. Due to racial name-calling and abuse, his life on the water turned ugly. Even though he still heard the call of new languages, foreign foods, and exotic cultures, Henson turned his back to the sea.

After Henson returned to Washington D.C. he settled for the relative safety and predictability that came with working as a store clerk. But the sea continued to call his name. One day Robert Peary, a young naval lieutenant in search of a sun helmet, wandered into the store where Henson worked. As he looked at hats, he shared with the store manager his desire to hire a manservant for an upcoming assignment in South America. Immediately the manager thought of Henson, who readily accepted this call of the wild.

The United States Navy had charged Peary with laying out a shipping route that would allow seagoing vessels from the Atlantic coastline to bypass South America on their way to the Pacific Ocean. For a year Lieutenant Peary and Henson lived and worked together in the jungles of Nicaragua. At some point, Peary added Henson to his land survey crew where Henson excelled in his added responsibilities. At the completion of their work, Henson and Peary returned to their respective corners of Washington, D.C.

Hungering for more adventure, Henson twice wrote to Peary offering his services. Peary did not respond to either letter. In the years to come, silence would become Peary's signature method of interacting with Henson at the conclusion of their exploits.

After trying his hands at a few unsatisfying jobs, Henson eventually returned to his old job as a store clerk. Peary who by then had been assigned to the League Island Navy Yard in Philadelphia wrote to Henson and inquired as to his interest in working at the Navy Yard as a messenger. Again, without hesitation, Henson turned in his stock apron and headed up the coast to Pennsylvania.

For nearly two years, Henson and Peary had little interaction, until Peary summoned Henson to his office. Was Henson available to serve as his manservant while he explored the North Pole? Unlike Navy Lt. Commander George W. DeLong, whose attempt to reach the North Pole resulted in his death and the deaths of 32 other seamen, Peary was confident his journey in search of the North Pole would be a success.

Henson was interested, but a few things had changed in his personal life. He now had a sweetheart—Eva Helen Flint—who was not keen on Henson leaving Philadelphia for parts unknown. Her parents were against his globetrotting as well. Henson felt the trip would provide him an opportunity to make history, even if the job only paid $50 a month. In the end, Eva gave her approval for Henson to follow his heart. The couple married two months before Henson departed for a tumultuous land of ice, wind, and snow. For the next twenty-two years, Henson would be Peary's most trusted and skilled first mate.

In 1886, on their initial trip to Greenland or what would become known as the North Greenland Expedition, Peary and Henson were accompanied by a support party of six that included Peary's wife Josephine and Frederick A. Cook, a medical doctor who would later proclaim that he was the first human to stand on the North Pole.

When the Peary party reached Greenland, the native Inuit people (Eskimos) were immediately attracted to Henson. Because of the warm color of his skin, the Inuit thought Henson was a long-lost native brother who had returned home. They quickly welcomed him into their world and gave Henson an Inuit name—Mahri-Pahluk—Matthew, the Kind One. Always curious and respectful of other cultures, Henson set about learning the Inuit language and its various dialects. As time moved on, Henson assumed interpretation duties between the Inuit and the Peary group. He also learned to ice fish, hunt reindeer, and musk oxen, and how to build sledges. Most importantly the Inuit taught Henson how to survive Greenland's harsh terrain, with its subzero temperatures that routinely dip to minus 50 degrees. From little tricks like using moss to insulate his boots, to building and driving a sledge powered by a team of eight to sixteen dogs, Henson learned all he could from the Inuit. On the other hand, Peary viewed the Inuit only as useful tools in his quest for the North Pole.

Even though Henson was the best sledge driver, when Peary set out on his trek toward the Pole, he chose another member of the team as his traveling companion. Henson was to remain at the base camp and attend to the needs of Josephine. When Peary returned, he lamented the fact that he was only able to travel about 500 miles before conditions forced him to end his journey. However, he did feel that in his travels he had reached the northernmost shore of the island.

Once back in America, Peary and Henson set about raising funds for their next trip to Greenland. In total the pair gave 165 presentations. Henson's role was to drive a pack of dogs onto the stage when Peary issued the call "Huk, huk" or Inuit for "go."

Peary returned to Greenland a year later with a party of eleven. Save for Peary's pregnant wife, only Peary, Henson, and another passenger possessed any viable exploration experience. From the beginning, this trip was plagued by misfortune and mishaps. Three of the crewmen were caught in a snow-storm while they tried to secure supplies on a glacier. Most of the team's fuel supply was lost in an accident. As the months went on, illness and injuries abounded. Finally, Peary decided to call a halt to expedition activities. When the *U.S.S. Falcon* arrived to return the crew to the United States, only Henson and a newspaper reporter named Hugh Lee answered the call for volunteers who would be willing to stay to salvage the expedition.

Eight months later, Peary, flanked by Henson and Lee, started out again for the North Pole. The trio did not have good luck. Each day their meager food supply continued to dwindle. Soon they were forced to slaughter and eat their sledge dogs. Their fate continued to worsen. A malnourished Lee was too weak to walk. The only source of food that remained was one dog. Somehow through 125-miles of blistering cold and blinding fog, Peary and Henson managed to pull a sledge, loaded with a near dead Lee, back to their camp. Henson pressed on to the closest Inuit settlement in search of help. Immediately, the Inuit began to nurse the starved and weaken explorers back to health. The experiences of this trip almost caused Henson to forever close his ears to the call of the wild. The only bright spot of the expedition may have been the Inuit orphan, Kudlooktoo, whom Henson had informally adopted.

In need of something besides failure to show for his efforts, Peary decided he would take back to America two giant meteorites the Inuits considered sacred. The meteorites were named Dog and Woman. The smaller meteorite, Dog, weighed a half-ton. Woman weighed three tons. Not satisfied, Peary came back the next year for a thirty-five-ton meteorite named Tent. Unsuc-cessful in his first attempt to pry Tent loose, Peary returned the following year with better equipment and, without permission of the Inuit, removed the colossal Tent. The American Museum of Natural History bought all three

Inuit artifacts for $40,000. That same year, Henson's wife Eva liberated herself from her absentee husband when she asked for and was granted a divorce.

A year later Peary, Henson, and just one other crew member, a doctor, launched another attempt for the Pole. This time they would start their trek from the northern Canadian island of Ellesmere. Six months into the expedition, Peary experienced the effects of extreme frostbite. When he removed his boots, the tips of eight of his toes snapped off. In the end, all eight toes required amputation.

During the next few years, Peary and Henson made a number of attempts to reach the Pole. Each time they were thwarted at the point where the surface ice ended, and the Arctic Sea began. To reach the North Pole, they needed the Arctic Sea to freeze into a solid surface onto which they could sledge across to the land mass surrounding the North Pole. There is only a small window of time when both the Arctic Sea and the land that abuts it are frozen at the same time. When would Peary and Henson find themselves at the sea, at the right time?

Eleven years had passed since Peary and Henson set out to reach the top of the world. Aside from the three meteorites housed at The American Museum of Natural History, there was little to show for their efforts. Was Henson wasting his life on a fool's errand? He had lost his marriage and had no children and very little money. Reaching the Pole was Peary's dream. What was his?

Three years would pass before Peary mounted another trip to the elusive Pole. Outfitted in a new ship, named in honor of President Theodore Roosevelt, Peary and Henson's hopes for success again were not realized. They did, however, manage to come within 174 miles of the Pole, the closest point they had ever reached. Also, during this trip, Henson's only child, an Inuit boy named Anaukaq was born.

The year following his son's birth, Henson remarried. His new wife brightened his outlook on life and supported Henson in his arctic adventures. Less than a year into his new marriage, Henson departed with Peary and two others headed again to the polar ice cap.

Henson and the other members of the party, which now included several Inuit families, established base camp on Ellesmere Island. As the team started

Matthew Alexander Henson

Public Domain Image. United States Library of Congress.

their ascent to the North Pole, they experienced unusually harsh conditions. The ice scape was dotted with unending ice fissures and pressure ridges of thin ice. The temperature was so low that the team had to continually beat their arms and legs to maintain blood circulation. Even the sledge dogs refused to move and had to be carried. Somehow the crusaders continued to advance closer to their prize.

Only 35 miles separated Peary, Henson, and four Inuit's—Ootah, Ooqueah, Egingwah, and Seegloo—from the Pole. Four hundred years of efforts by numerous men had come down to this moment.

Still suffering from his toe amputations, Peary instructed Henson to proceed forward and break a path for their triumphant arrival at the Pole. Giddy with the reality that success was at hand, Henson drove his sledge fast and hard. In an instant he found himself facing death. The thin ice beneath him had broken. Henson, his sledge, and his team of dogs were all thrown into the arctic waters. With the quickness of an eagle, Ootah swooped in and pulled Henson to safety. Henson was able to continue the march forward in part due to his clothing. His bearskin pants were lined with flannel that absorbed water. They also were overlaid by an additional band of bearskin. His torso was protected by a flannel shirt and hooded deerskin coat. Like his Inuit companions, his boots and mittens were crafted from sealskin and lined with inserts made from polar bear fur.

Another four hours would pass before Henson intuitively felt that he, Ootah, and Ooqueah had reached the North Pole. When Peary arrived, he pulled out his sextant which showed a reading of 89°57' as close a reading as his equipment could measure to 90° which represents true north or the North Pole. As opposed to elation, Peary was furious. Henson's footprints had touched the North Pole before his!

After surveying the surrounding area, Peary fixed an American flag onto one of the igloos Henson and the Inuit had built. After that Peary went inside the igloo and went to sleep. On the trip back to the base camp, Peary gave Henson the silent treatment, which he would more or less continue until his death ten years later.

While Peary and Henson were in their last pursuit of the North Pole, Dr. Frederick A. Cook, a member of their first Greenland exploration party, claimed he had reached the North Pole a year before Peary. Cook's claim forced Peary to defend his right to the title of being first. Geographic societies and the U.S. Congress examined evidence in an attempt to determine the validity of the competing claims. In the end, Peary's evidence proved more substantial than that of Cook. After the dispute died down, Peary received numerous awards and honors and his naval rank was upgraded to Captain. Within a short period, he obtained another promotion to Rear Admiral and retired with a hefty pension.

On the other hand, the general public viewed Henson as just another domestic servant. Unlike Peary, he did not receive any medals or awards. He could not even find a decent job and ended up working at a parking lot as a car jockey. Once word of Henson's plight spread through the black community, Booker T. Washington and other Black leaders hosted an appreciation banquet in his honor. They also were successful in securing "a good government job" for Henson at the U.S. Custom House in New York. It was the same job he had eighteen years before at the League Island Navy Yard in Philadelphia. He would again be a messenger.

It would take almost another thirty-five years for Henson to begin to garner the type of recognition afforded to Peary. Even then, when the Navy presented medals to Peary's last crew, Henson was not allowed to participate in the main ceremony. He received his medal in a separate room.

However, as social norms changed, Henson and his contributions gained wider acknowledgement. On the forty-fifth anniversary of Peary and Henson's arrival at the North Pole, President Eisenhower honored Henson at a White House reception. Peary most assuredly would have been miffed.

"…we often forget that life is an ongoing adventure…"
Maya Angelou, American Poet and Memorialist

Matthew Alexander Henson
Audacity Principle: Adaptability

Matthew Henson loved life. He loved adventure. And most of all he loved people. By age 13 Matthew was pretty much on his own. Both of his parents and an uncle, who had stepped in to raise him, were dead. Faced with so much loss at a young age, some children choose the safety of familiarity to cope, but not Henson. He thrived on the unknown.

Free of his most significant familial ties, a thrill-seeking Henson made his way from Washington, D.C., to the Port of Baltimore where he opened himself to the mysteries of the sea. For five years he visited the four corners of the world and bathed in the unique, but strikingly similar, slices of life he found at each port of call. There were differences in the languages and dialects that tickled his ears, in the foods upon which his eyes and tongue feasted, and the aroma and smells his nose inhaled. But there also was a sameness in the welcoming smiles of strangers, the hardened muscles of men at work, and the laughter of small children. When Henson waved goodbye to the sea and thanked the world for the lessons it had taught him, he felt ready to settle into the routine duties and obligations of a respectable young man. That is until the world and its many cultures came calling again for his heart.

Over a 22-year period, Henson made seven trips to then uncharted interior of the Arctic in his quest to sit at the top of the world. Along the way he completely opened himself to the native Inuit culture and its people. By allowing himself to be vulnerable, he not only achieved his goal, he also soaked in layer upon layer of newfound knowledge about what makes us human. He came to see the beauty of the human soul and gained a clearer understanding of community. He also more deeply understood the sacredness of the human experience. Henson's most cherished memories were those made with the nomadic Inuit whose culture was a profound sacrament to the joy of life and the love for one's fellow man.

If Henson's initial interaction with the Inuit would have echoed that of his employer Robert Peary, the probability of the duo surviving their first trip to the Arctic would have been quite low. For when you attempt to hide your ignorance and vulnerabilities, you dishonor not only others, but yourself as well. We cannot play by only our rules. Like a river, life flows at its best when it is not artificially dammed by closed-mind requirements that it come only in the size, style, or model of a particular choosing. When people are insensitive to the distinctiveness of others, they miss out on gifts others stand ready to give, because of their ego, arrogance, or self-importance.

Often a person's fear of the unknown causes them to invent reasons to severely restrict their interactions. Never crowd your mind with self-limiting beliefs as to what is possible and what you are capable of accomplishing. Refuse to tell yourself that you are not enough, or that your days for engaging the world in new ways are over. Skip trying to convince yourself that you are too old, too tired, or too afraid to enjoy the endless possibilities of the human experience available outside your self-made prison. When you step out of your comfort zone ready to try out new experiences, you add to your understanding of yourself, world, and the people in it.

Ninety percent of what humans fear never materializes, and thus should not control the size of the world from which you derive meaning. Small boxes are pretty cases for rings, but not for the boundaries of your lives. Your choice to remain closed or open to life are like muscles. The more you make certain choices, the stronger and easier those choices become. When you are open, adaptable, and comfortable with the unexpected, you are free to push through any boundaries in your life. New worlds of wonder are awaiting your arrival. Are you ready to explore the beauty of the unknown?

###

"A wise man adapts himself to circumstances as water shapes itself to the vessel that contains it."

Anonymous

Matthew Alexander Henson Resources

BOOKS
A Negro Explorer at the North Pole: The Autobiography of Matthew Henson
Matthew Henson
(Cahners Business Information, Inc., 2001)

Grade Levels: 2-3
Keep On!: The Story of Matthew Henson, Co-Discoverer of the North Pole
Deborah Hopkinson
(Peachtree Publishing Company; Reprint edition, 2015)

Grade Levels: 3-9
Matthew Henson Arctic Adventurer (Graphic Biographies)
B. A. Hoena
(Capstone Press, 2006)

Grade Levels: 5-8
Onward
Dolores Johnson
(National Geographic Society, 2006)

ONLINE SITES
matthewhenson.com
biography.com/explorer/matthew-henson
blackpast.org/african-american-history/henson-matthew-1866-1955/

YOU TUBE VIDEOS
Susanna 20 Channel: Matthew Henson Discovers the North Pole
Woodrow Wilson Center: Discovering Matthew Henson

SITES AND MEMORIALS TO VISIT

Maryland State House Rotunda (Memorial Plaque)
100 State Circle
Annapolis, MD 21401

Burial Site:
Arlington National Cemetery
Arlington, VA

8. SAVORY

Lena Paul Richard
September 11, 1892–November 27, 1950

Lena tried without much success to find a comfortable spot in which she could rest both her suitcase and her legs. After talking with other Blacks who had traveled up North, she started her trip to Boston, Massachusetts with the knowledge that the train car to which she was assigned was of lesser quality than the cars afforded white passengers. But this cramped and restricted space was ridiculous, and it would be almost 1,000 miles before she experienced any relief. Lena understood that once she arrived in Washington, D.C., she would switch to a non-segregated train for the last leg of her trip to the Bay state. But it sure would be nice if she could store her suitcase in a luggage rack or have access to a more spacious restroom, right now.

As she thought about the trip ahead, Lena still wondered why Mrs. Vairin wanted her to go to yet another cooking class. Since her early teens, during school breaks, Lena had worked alongside both her mother and aunt for the well-connected and prominent Vairin family. After Mrs. Vairin realized Lena's gift and passion for cooking, she reassigned the budding chef to kitchen duty and even paid for Lena to attend local cooking schools to expand her culinary knowledge.

All of Mrs. Vairin's lady friends raved about Lena's tasty lunches, dinners, and desserts, and some even tried to sweet talk the food wiz away from the Vairin family. As Lena continued to think, she vaguely remembered seeing a copy of *The Boston Cooking-School Cook Book* in the Vairin house, but she never felt a need to read or use it. Then Mrs. Vairin asked her if she would like to attend the famous Miss Fannie Farmer's School of Cookery in Boston. Lena didn't think the school could teach her much more than she already knew, but Mrs. Vairin kept talking about standardization of recipes and serving sizes. Of course, her mother and aunt were quite proud of the opportunities she had been given, but Lena wondered what they would say about this miserable train ride.

Although the founder of Miss Farmer's School of Cookery, Fannie Farmer had died nearly three years prior to Lena's arrival, the school continued to turn out well-trained cooks. While many of her classmate's kitchen skills were elementary when compared to her abilities, Lena did come to understand the importance of using agreed upon standards in place of a pinch of this and a sprinkling of that. Two ounces in California equaled two ounces in Wisconsin, and five teaspoons of oil in Chicago should yield the same amount of oil in Miami. During the two months she was in Boston, Lena also became intrigued by the increasing number of her classmates who expressed their desire to learn the basics of Creole cooking. Most of her peers had heard about New Orleans' savory food, but few had actually tasted any. Without hesitation Lena shared a few tips and tricks, but soon realized that a new kind of opportunity might be hers for the taking. Perhaps she could become a self-made food ambassador.

When Lena returned to New Orleans later in 1918, she cooked a few new dishes for the Vairin family, but she spent almost all of her free time thinking of ways she could use her Boston experience to better the Black community. She knew some of her Farmer School classmates were European immigrants who hoped what they learned would help them obtain jobs as cooks. Maybe she could open a school for Blacks that would prepare them for culinary success. Unlike housekeeping or landscaping, cooking allowed for creativity, job satisfaction, and paid a higher wage. Most people who have an interest in cooking possess some level of skill that needs a small bit of refining and expansion. Lena was convinced she could uplift members of her community by teaching them in-demand job skills. Given that Lena was a young black woman in her twenties with a lot of ideas but not much financial backing, nearly two decades would pass before she amassed the resources needed to open and operate a cooking school. In the meantime, Lena married Percival Richard and gave birth to her only child Marie. She also started the laborious task of developing a creole cookbook.

Creole is a style of cuisine that combines ingredients prevalent in West African, indigenous American, French, and Spanish cooking. Some creole dishes also showcase Sicilian, Irish, and Caribbean influences. Louisiana creole food originally was prepared for wealthy New Orleanians who could afford to purchase ingredients such as okra, tomatoes, and cayenne pepper in the 18th century. During its heyday in the 1840s, New Orleans ranked third among U.S. cities in total population and held the distinction as wealthiest city in America. These bragging rights resulted in part from the operation of America's largest domestic slave market and third largest port, in terms of inbound international tonnage. Though its financial fortunes declined with the end of slavery, New Orleans' reputation for flavorful food endured.

In 1937 Lena realized her dream of opening a cooking school for the youth of her community. A side bonus to operating her school was the opportunity to test some of the 300 creole recipes worthy of her name and reputation. Recipes for standards such as gumbo, a brown or red colored seafood or meat soup served over rice, or bread pudding were easy to standardize and write. However other local favorites such as Baked Alaska and Stuffed Crawfish Shells required more time to perfect. Her school provided a large ready-made laboratory in which she could determine if her more involved recipes could be easily understood by novice cooks. Finally, at the close of the 1930s or twenty-one years after she had graduated from the renowned Miss Fanny Farmer's School of Cookery, Lena self-published *Lena Richard's Cook Book*.

Lena did not pretend to originate all the recipes in her encyclopedia of creole cooking. She graciously acknowledged the contributions of the many African-American cooks who unselfishly shared their knowledge and wisdom of cooking with her. Hoping for some level of literary success, Lena was ecstatic when local customers began to buy multiple copies of her book as gifts

Lena Paul Richard

Image courtesy of The John & Bonnie Boyd Hospitality & Culinary Collection, Southern Food and Beverage Museum.

for out-of-state friends and family. Soon orders were coming in by the hundreds and before she knew it, her book had caught the eye and palettes of cooking's Who's Who. Both Clementine Paddleford, a nationally recognized newspaper and magazine food writer, and James Beard, a celebrated chef and cooking school entrepreneur were smitten by her work. Paddleford advocated for powerhouse publisher Houghton Mifflin to re-publish and market Lena's cookbook. The following year, the *Lena Richard's Cook Book* was reissued nationally by Houghton Mifflin as the *New Orleans Cook Book*, albeit without the dignified image of Lena that graced the original compilation of New Orleans dishes. That same year Lena also accepted an offer to become chef at the nearly 180 years old, Bird and Bottle Inn located in Garrison, New York.

As the 1940s progressed, Lena continued to expand her culinary reach and growing national reputation. After opening her own New Orleans restaurant in 1941, *Lena's Eatery*, the famed cook received another out-of-state call for her services. This time the request came from Colonial Williamsburg, Virginia, a historic district backed by John D Rockefeller. Lena accepted the position of head chef at the historic district's internationally renowned Travis House Restaurant and Inn. Again, Lena packed her bags and started on her second Creole cooking ambassadorship. After a few years of preparing meals for luminaries such as Clementine and Mary Churchill, wife and daughter of British Prime Minister Winston Churchill, Lena returned to New Orleans in 1945 and began her next entrepreneurial venture, a frozen food company.

Working with local co-packer, Bordelon Fine Foods, Lena was able to send heat-and-eat prepared meals to legions of enthusiastic fans and foodies. But Lena's most innovative and forward-looking foray into the lucrative world of satisfying most people's desire for tasty food still was ahead of her.

In 1948 television was in its infancy. At an average price of $400, the equivalent of more than $4,000 in 2019, only a mere 35,000 televisions had been sold across the nation. However, New Orleans native sons, Edgar B. Stern Sr. and namesake Edgar B Stern, Jr. believed New Orleans would be a prime market for the newest form of broadcast communication, the nascent television. A few days before the 1948 Christmas season, the visionary Sterns flipped the switch to broadcast on WDSU television station. By 1949, one of the channel's local stars was Lena Richard.

Before Julia Childs, Rachelle Ray, or the Food Network, Lena Richard hosted a twice weekly cooking show that was must-see-tv for New Orleans elites. In a conversational and confidence building tone, Lena walked viewers through recipes that were both praiseworthy and crowd favorites. Lena's show aired seven years before the famed *Nat "King" Cole Show* and long before African-Americans could freely exercise their basic civil rights i.e., walking through front doors, voting, or sitting in whatever seat they chose.

Sadly, Lena died in 1950 from a sudden heart attack following a live broadcast of her show. Though cut down in her prime, Lena's enthusiasm for life and cooking endures in the memories and the taste buds of those who were nourished by her divine meals. Her written record serves as a beacon for today's culinary icons of color who may not know the path she lit for their success.

###

"My purpose in opening a cooking school was to teach men and women the art of food preparation and serving in order that they would become capable of preparing and serving food for any occasion and also that they might be in a position to demand higher wages."

Lena Richard
Celebrity chef and serial entrepreneur

Lena Paul Richard
Audacity Principle: Ujima

Because of her culinary talents and skills Lena Richard had visceral access to the upper echelons of American society. She could have easily been seduced into thinking that there was only room for herself in the lofty world to which her cooking skills allowed her access. But even as a young woman in her twenties, Lena's thinking identified her as a 20th century "Race Woman."

Since their arrival in America, Blacks have been stereotyped and viewed by large segments of society as all things negative from inferior and unworthy to contemptable and undeserving. Forced to live as second-class citizens and denied basic human dignity, many Blacks viewed the successes and accomplishments of other African-Americans as a collective victory for all. Race men and women expanded this concept to include a race consciousness or solidarity where they dedicated themselves not only to their personal ascension, but to a commitment to lift others as they climbed. Lena dedicated herself to memorializing the contributions of the nameless Black cooks that melded together the different food traditions of European, Indigenous American, and West African cultures into Louisiana Creole Cuisine. In the preface to *Lena Richard's Cook Book*, she not only took a victory lap for herself, but for the thousands of unnamed Black female kitchen magicians and artists whose talents helped establish the South's hospitality profile.

The first observance and celebration of African-American culture, known as Kwanzaa, occurred sixteen years following Lena Richard's death. Kwanzaa begins the day after Christmas and concludes New Year's Day. Each day during this week-long observance, the seven principles of African heritage are celebrated and collectively referred to as the NGUZO-SABA. Lena Richard was the embodiment of the third principle Kwanzaa—Ujima (oo-JEE-mah) or collective work and responsibility.

Lena witnessed firsthand the limited job opportunities available to young African-American New Orleanians. During Lena's childhood, when Blacks sought economic opportunities outside of the South, many were intimidated into not leaving. Reportedly one New Orleans' mayor made a formal request to the president of the Illinois Central Railroad to deny passage to Blacks on all northbound trains leaving the city. The loss of their cheap labor would have been an economic gut-punch.

Most of the jobs reserved for Blacks allowed for little inventiveness, paid paltry wages, and required backbreaking work. Lena thought if she could pass on to her younger neighbors the knowledge and information she had been privileged to learn, they too might improve their circumstances through hospitality jobs. Why should they spend 30–40 years of their lives limited to only washing pots and pans or sweeping floors? Even if they couldn't find or create employment for themselves, they could move out West or relocate to the East Coast.

Lena, however, didn't just think about doing something, she actually worked toward creation of opportunities for the youth of her community. As she advanced her personal goals, she provided employment opportunities for community members in her various eateries and catering businesses. When she had amassed enough capital to open her cooking school, she had the necessary business skills to weather any lean periods. For ten years, Lena poured her energy and passion into shaping a new generation of African-American culinary movers and shakers.

Do you see inequality of access to a better life as a burden for only those caught in the spirals of ignorance or poverty? Are you willing to practice the concept of Ujima throughout the year and not just during Kwanzaa? What knowledge, skills or abilities do you possess that your community may need? Lightening another's load does not require grand plans or actions. Something as simple as teaching others how to present themselves is information that is needed and can contribute to a life of independence. Offering a few hours of babysitting to a single mom suggests recognition of her struggle and that you are cheering her toward success.

How magnificent would each of our legacies shine if we patterned our lives after that of the sequoia. Documented as the largest trees on earth, the typical sequoia is taller than a 25-story building. Surprisingly, a sequoia possesses a shallow root system that may only grow about 20 feet deep. How can this tree with an average life span of 3,000 years remain upright through centuries of weather perils? The answer lies in their interconnected root structures. Unlike many tree species, sequoia's grow in groves, not alone. The inter-connectivity of their stubby root systems allows for communal strength, support and inter-dependence. In other words, Ujima.

"It takes a village to raise a child"

African proverb

Lena Paul Richard Additional Resources

BOOKS

New Orleans Cook Book

Lena Richard

Houghton Mifflin company; Early Edition (January 1, 1940)

WEBSITES

AmericanHistory.si.edu

CeroleGlen.org

Colonial Williamsburg.org

NationalMuseumofAmericanHistory.org

PODCAST

si.edu/sidedoor "Lena Richard: America's Unknown Celebrity Chef"

John Carter Washington
Circa 1921–January 24, 2017

and

Lyda Moore Merrick
November 19, 1890–February 14, 1987

Providence did not smile on John Carter Washington. Born without eyeballs and ears that barely worked, John's last moments with his sick and dying mother had been in a Durham, North Carolina back alley. Without any relatives or family friends to provide care, John became a ward of Durham's African-American Lincoln Hospital. As baby John continued to grow, he was moved to an orphanage, then placed in the Durham County Home, a facility for the poor and disabled. Along the way, instead of finding love, John reaped abuse in the form of corporal punishment and cruel pranks.

North Carolina was the first state to provide funding for the education of Black children who were blind and/or deaf. However, in 1926 when five-year-old John enrolled as a student in the residential Colored Department of the North Carolina Institution for the Education of the Deaf and Dumb and the Blind (NCIEDDB), his fortunes did not improve. With a naturally inquisitive mind, John soon got tired of the school's heavy emphasis on vocational training at the expense of academic development. After so many years of learning shoe repair, broom assembly, and mattress stuffing, John began to express dissatisfaction with his education. Known for his supposedly rebellious attitude and poor grades, John dished out what he most often received, negativity. Finally fed up with his pushback, aggression, and troublemaking, school officials showed a teenage John the door. No longer a charge of the state, John would have to figure out how to make it on his own.

Once he had secured a new place to live, John turned his attention toward filling some of the academic shortfalls of his years at NCIEDDB. To improve his usage of the English language, he enrolled in a grammar course offered by the Hadley Correspondence School, which provided free academic courses for the blind. He also made his first independent trip outside of North Carolina to Chicago, Illinois. Though John was now in a city that was much bigger and had a faster lifestyle than Durham, he set about making a way for himself in his new temporary home. He learned how to negotiate his way among the throngs of city folk who choked the sidewalks and crossways. He also applied himself fully to his studies at the College of Swedish Massage. John used every bit of frustration, determination, and imagination he experienced or possessed to succeed. More than anything else, his commitment to a life that did not involve his pathetically standing on a sidewalk, supported by a white cane in his right hand and a can of pencils in his left, was rock solid. He would not spend his days hoping for someone to toss a coin of pity his way. He journeyed to Chicago for one thing—skills that would allow him to stand on his own as a man. He, and no one else, would be responsible for his life.

Upon completion of his course of study and the receipt of his professional credentials in the art of massage, which attested to his bodywork expertise, a maturing John returned to Durham as a man, ready to take on adult responsibilities. After he landed a job at the local YMCA, John eventually took a wife, and started a family of his own. He was definitely a man's man.

On the other hand, most people considered Lyda Moore Merrick an aristocrat. Her father, Dr. Aaron McDuffie Moore, the first Black physician in Durham, North Carolina, either created or was a partner in several successful businesses. In addition to owning a pair of local drugstores, Dr. Moore was a principal in what were to become two of America's oldest and most lucrative Black-owned-and-operated financial institutions—North Carolina Mutual Life Insurance Company and Mechanics and Farmers Bank. He also spearheaded the establishment of Lincoln Hospital and School of Nursing, which provided medical care and education to area Blacks.

By all accounts, Dr. Moore was an avid reader who revered books and believed that within their pages lied the power to change lives. To this end, he established a reading room for Durham's Black citizens in the basement of White Rock Baptist Church where he and his family worshiped. He also outfitted it with nearly 800 books that ranged from the classics to the sciences. This donation became the nucleus of the Durham Colored Library. It was at the Colored Library that his daughter Lyda would receive the inspiration for what would become her most important and enduring legacy.

As children of privilege, Lyda and her sister, Mattie Louise, attended the best private colleges and universities—historically black Fisk University and Ivy League Columbia University. Upon completion of their studies in New York, Dr. Moore treated his daughters to a month-long cross-country train trip to San Francisco, California. There the family took in the sites and wonders of the 1915 World's Fair. A year later, Lyda married Edward R. Merrick, the son of North Carolina Mutual founder John Merrick. Their wedding was one of the most talked about social events of the year with luminaries such as civil rights activist Dr. W. E. B. DuBois and the mayor of Durham and his wife in attendance.

As a young wife and mother, Lyda's days revolved around her two daughters, music, and art. When she was not providing private piano lessons or drawing, she enjoyed singing in both the North Carolina Mutual's glee club and quartet. And like her father, she also enjoyed the company of a good book.

When Lyda's children were preschoolers, Lincoln Hospital, the medical facility started by her father, caught fire. The resulting flames and thick smoke required the evacuation of all patients—including the motherless, blind, and partially deaf baby boy—John Carter Washington. Like other members of the community who assisted in caring for the evacuees, Lyda welcomed baby John into her home. Lyda had no idea how this one act of kindness would significantly influence the course of her civic life. For the next sixty-five years Lyda and John enjoyed a mutually rewarding friendship that ultimately would impact the lives of thousands.

As a young adult, John was instrumental in Lyda's advocating for the establishment of a library resource center and club for the blind at the Durham Colored Library.

After the library opened its Corner for the Blind which was stocked with audio recordings and Braille reading materials, Lyda spent many hours either reading to or providing other services to the center's customers. A few years later, John, perhaps thinking about the holes in his K-12 education, asked Lyda if she could find a way to help those without access to the Corner of the Blind learn more about Black culture and life in the larger Black community. He thought that, rather than reading to the blind, Lyda and he should start a magazine that blind citizens could read for themselves. Always open to new ideas, Lyda soon felt that such a magazine could serve as a useful bridge between the blind and the sighted world.

For more than a year, Lyda worked with John to bring his most impactful request to life. Without any specialized training in magazine production or management, and without any real budget, Lyda worked exhaustively to get the first issue of the *Negro Braille Magazine* ready for its debut. First, research on the size of the potential subscription base and braille printing was required. Also, operational questions such as frequency of publication, postal regulations, and mailing costs needed to be answered. Editorial decisions concerning the types and sizes of articles for each edition, along with a fundraising plan, had to be developed. It was during this pre-production phase when Lyda learned that the federal government would pay for postage. And John Johnson, who would go on to publish *Ebony* and *Jet* magazines, granted Ldya and John permission to reproduce, for free, articles from his *Negro Digest*.

When the 78-page first edition of the *Negro Braille Magazine* rolled off the press, it was hard to tell who was prouder, Lyda or John Washington. Now the blind could read about the lives and activities of Black newsmakers, entertainers, historical figures, and athletes. As word spread about the magazine, requests for subscriptions came from such far-flung countries as Malaysia, Australia, and Scotland. For the next 18 years, Lyda served as the magazine's editor and chief fundraiser, while John held down the post of associate editor. On more than one occasion, Lyda's husband financially sponsored the free quarterly publication. During one particularly rough patch, CBS Evening News aired a story about Lyda and John's work and the need for financial donations.

In 1969, operating costs per issue were about $1,000. That same year, the average cost of a four-door sedan was about $2,500. Building a solid financial foundation for the publication remained a persistent challenge, but readership continued to grow.

When Lyda turned over leadership of the magazine, John continued in his role as associate editor. As the magazine celebrated milestone anniversaries, John was ever present, guiding its continual growth and development. He also maintained his massage career, raised three daughters and kept the flames of romance lit in his 55-year marriage to Fanny Ruth Washington, who also happened to be blind.

Nearly 100 years after Lyda and John Washington began their lifelong connection, the *Negro Braille Magazine* (now named *The Merrick/Washington Magazine for the Blind*) remains the only national publication dedicated to the needs of blind African-Americans. No doubt Dr. Aaron McDuffie Moore would be proud not only of his eldest daughter's life of service, but that of John Washington as well.

###

"The ends you serve that are selfish will take you no further than yourself but the ends you serve that are for all, in common, will take you into eternity."

Marcus Mosiah Garvey

Jamaican political activist

John Carter Washington and Lyda Moore Merrick holding copy of Negro Braille Magazine.

Image courtesy of North Carolina Collection, Durham County Library.

John Carter Washington and Lyda Moore Merrick
Audacity Principle: Service to Others

John Washington may not have been born with eyeballs, but his mind saw everything. He saw how society's view of those with disabilities had not changed much since the Victorian Age. He and those like him were either objects of pity or victims of ridicule. Even the President of the United States, Franklin D. Roosevelt, who was permanently paralyzed from the waist down, was embarrassed and ashamed of his disability. Not John. He was determined to play the hand fate dealt him and use his life for something greater than himself— service to others.

When John was a child, he spoke as a child. He wanted whatever he wanted, when he wanted it. If he could not talk his teachers into offering him more in the way of education that exceeded the bundling of straws into brooms or the re-caning of chairs, then he would take his loud protests to the Governor of North Carolina. Never mind that his protests resulted in his swift removal from school and the institutional housing that came with it. Because he stretched the socially ordained boundaries for the handicapped (the polite, but judgmental, descriptive term for those with marked physical limitations) beyond prescribed limits, John found himself, well, homeless.

Given a lifeline by way of the Chicago College of Swedish Massage, John quickly moved from man-child to full adulthood. In the big city, where he was alone and without much community support, John quickly matured. It was do or die time, and he *did*. He also began to think and plan for his true calling—being a clarion voice for the physically challenged. After John returned to Durham, he set about the work of most 20-somethings—establishment of his career and family. He also transformed from a teen rebel into an adult advocate determined to move the needs of disabled citizens into the forefront of community concerns.

It is amazing how John found time to serve others, unlike many who think they do not have time for anything or anyone outside of their immediate families. They self-limit the service that may be theirs to give through the intonation of phrases such as "Sorry, maybe next year" or "When I get a few hours to spare, I'll volunteer," etc. For John, the problems he spoke to were now, not tomorrow, thus his service was needed in the present, not the future.

For as lively and as energetically as John embraced life, his maturity was undergirded by a spirit of humility. He knew Lyda Moore Merrick's lifelong concern and love for him was genuine. He only wished he could share with others some of the intellectual gifts she had given him. Because of her father's material wealth, she had been privileged not only to go to college, but to an Ivy League graduate school as well. The material wealth of her husband had afforded her opportunities to travel, to express her fondness for the arts, and to assume leadership positions in civic affairs. She graciously shared the bounty of her life experiences with John and worked to improve services for him and her other sightless neighbors. Could he dare ask her to do more?

Lyda Moore Merrick was a servant leader long before the 1970s term was coined. She showed her concern and care by putting people first. As she listened to understand others, she did so with both her ears and her heart. Although her father summed up his philosophy of life in different terms, Lyda accepted without question the axiom, "Our service is the rent we pay for living."

When an infant John was brought to her home following a fire at Durham's Lincoln Hospital, she did not view him with pity or reproach. She knew that, given the right opportunities, he too could unlock whatever potential and creativity that existed inside his soft little body.

Through the years she advocated on his behalf and watched and waited as all adult cheerleaders do to see what gifts their "special young person" will share with the world. And John did not disappoint; whatever he wanted for himself, he wanted the same for members of his community. So, when he asked Lyda to put together a braille magazine that emphasized Black culture, she did not see his request as outrageous, but rather as an opportunity for John to shine his light brighter and farther.

As a team, with Lyda as editor and John as associate editor, the sightless were introduced to the beauty of the Black experience along with relevant information related to the management of their disability. In their world, color was not the first characteristic by which they judged others. Their need for functional improvements to their lives and the maximum development of their minds mattered more than the hue of someone else's skin. Perhaps this is why the *Negro Braille Magazine* found an international audience. The most enduring fruit of John and Lyda's lifelong friendship continues to this day. Because they gave their hands to service, their literary baby, now known as *The Merrick/Washington Magazine for the Blind,* continues to expand and enrich the lives of readers around the world. When you serve others with compassion, empathy, and understanding, you will always receive more than you give. When you meet the needs of others, you meet your own needs as well. Ask any reader of *The Merrick/Washington Magazine for the Blind.*

"Do your little bit of good where you are; it's those little bits of good put together that overwhelm the world."

Desmond Tutu
South African Anglican Cleric and Theologian

John Carter Washington and Lyda Moore Merrick Resources

BOOK
A Gift of Love: The Negro Braille Magazine Story
Delores Marvin Towles
(The Merrick-Washington Magazine for the Blind Project, 1985)

ONLINE SITES
andjusticeforall.dconc.gov
durhamcountylibrary.org

SITES AND MEMORIALS TO VISIT
Lydia Moore Merrick Community Room
Hayti Heritage Center/St Joseph's Historic Foundation
804 Old Fayetteville Street
Durham, NC 27701

Sanford L. Warren Library
1201 Fayetteville Street
Durham, NC 27707

Burial Site (John Carter Washington):
Mt. Gilead Orange Baptist Church Cemetery
3512 Pleasant Green Road
Durham, NC 27705

Burial Site (Lydia Moore Merrick):
Beechwood Cemetery
3300 Fayetteville Street
Durham, NC 27707

10. GODFATHER

John Charles Robinson
November 26, 1905–March 27, 1954

A young John Robinson squinted at the sky. A man riding the air was moving closer and closer to John and the waters that bordered Gulfport, Mississippi. How could the man and his machine stay in the air? John wondered if the man was real or a ghost.

When the "King of Aviation" John Moisant stepped from his plane onto the beach, the younger John Robinson stood in silent awe along with the other onlookers. Moisant looked like any other man, save the white scarf around his neck and giant goggles that covered half of his face and eyes. But what allowed him to leave the earth and move around the sky? Robinson was still lost in thoughts of the mysterious Moisant when the daredevil aviator climbed back into his plane and rose into a blanket of clouds. As John watched Moisant and his plane disappear, he told himself that when he grew up, he too would possess the same power to ride the wind.

John was fortunate in that he was raised by parents who had high hopes for his and his sister Bertha's future. When he completed Gulfport's High School for the Colored, his parents enrolled him in Booker T. Washington's Tuskegee Institute where he studied automotive mechanics. There John's natural talents were on full display, especially when he completed the graduation requirement of building a car from the ground up.

At age 18, John was a college graduate looking for a job and a way into the world of aviation. Fully aware that he needed to leave the South to realize his dreams, John moved to Detroit, Michigan. Known as the Motor City, Detroit was home to various car manufacturers and Lockheed Aviation's parent company, Detroit Aircraft.

John's leap into the Motor City's job market mirrored that of his experience in Gulfport. Initially he only received job offers for menial, low-skilled jobs that required more muscle than brains. After a bit of time, he found work as an auto repairman, which allowed him to showcase his mechanical chops. Within a short period of time, John was named head mechanic and given supervisory responsibilities for six other white coworkers. This accomplishment was noteworthy, given the racial caste system of 1920's America. In most relationships involving blacks and whites, blacks did not occupy positions of authority.

In his spare time, John continued to dream about becoming a pilot. He studied aircraft mechanics and kept abreast of the latest developments in the ever-changing world of aviation. When the day finally arrived for his first flight, John knew a lot more about the mechanics of airplanes than the average passenger.

John's first flight involved turbulence though not from the air, instead it was racial hostility.

Responding to an advertisement for plane rides, John made his way out to the countryside that surrounded Detroit. However, when he attempted to buy the ticket for his first ride, the pilot refused to take his money. Upon hearing the same pilot discuss a mechanical issue in a different plane, John offered to fix the problem in exchange for a ride. The pilot of the crippled plane agreed to the deal, though after John repaired the plane, he was still unable to secure a plan ride.

Another pilot, who had watched John's fruitless attempts to obtain passage, stepped in and offered John his first view of life from the sky. As the plane began to leave the ground, John experienced a case of nerves, then he settled down and soaked in the majesty of all that lay below.

When John asked his pilot to give him flying lessons, the benevolent pilot refused, citing the racial codes that governed most interactions between the races. The pilot did, however, offer some useful advice. He suggested that, if John was serious about learning how to fly, he should apply for admission to the prestigious Curtiss Wright Aeronautical Flight School located in Chicago, Illinois.

Within a year, John left Detroit for Chicago.

After John landed a mechanics job with Chicago's Yellow Cab Company, his technical skills and pleasant personality again impressed his employer and co-workers. He also met another young Black man equally as smitten with aircrafts—Cornelius Robinson Coffey. Whenever time permitted, John and Cornelius worked on turning a car engine into an airplane engine for use on their first aircraft. Their plan was not a wishful dream. Aviation was still in its infancy, and many pilots built or modified parts for their planes; however, instead of utilizing the repurposed car engine, John and Cornelius installed a transformed motorcycle engine into their first plane—a WACO 9. More than ever, John was determined to earn a pilot's license.

In between getting married and managing his own auto mechanics shop, John pursued every opportunity to trade his mechanical know-how for the use of various other aircrafts. Finally, he reached the required number of flight hours needed to earn his private pilot's license. Many years had passed since John first saw the "King of Aviation's" plane crack the Mississippi sky. When he was awarded a private pilot license—No. 26,042—John again felt the magic of that long-ago day in Gulfport.

With license in hand, an enthusiastic John applied for admission to the Curtiss-Wright Aeronautical Flight School. When he showed up on the first day of class, his admission was cancelled. Again, the barrier of race stood in his way. Not one to be deterred, John demanded to see the school's president. After a number of conversations with the president, in which John's passion and knowledge demonstrated his commitment, his admission was reinstated.

But there was a catch. John would have to work as the school's weekend janitor, and whatever knowledge he soaked up while he performed his cleaning duties was his. Interestingly, Tuskegee's Booker T. Washington also gained admission to his alma mater, Hampton Institute, by way of a broom handle. Like Washington, John probably reasoned that one foot in is better than two feet out. As he performed his janitorial duties, John eavesdropped on lessons, copied material left on blackboards, and read lecture notes he happened to find on the desk of instructors. This arrangement however did not last long. John soon received permission to exchange his dust rag for a pencil as a full-fledged student. Two years later, John Charles Robinson graduated at the top of his class with a hard-won master mechanic of aviation certification.

Always interested in the advancement of his community, John lobbied Curtiss-Wright to admit more Black students. Like a dripping faucet, John finally wore down the president's resistance to his arguments. If John could come up with 25 students, the school would open its doors to Blacks. After months of recruiting, giving lectures, showing films, and canvasing house to house, John delivered 25 students.

In turn, Curtiss-Wright hired John as an assistant instructor in an effort to reduce any blow-back from other students and faculty. From this initial group of 25 students, eight graduated. Two of the eight were women—Janet Harmon Bragg, a registered nurse, and Willa Beatrice Brown, a social worker. Notably, after John's first year as an instructor, the restriction, whereby he was only to teach Black students, was lifted.

During this same period, the Acres Airport, from which John did most of his flying and repair work, closed. None of the other local airports were interested in servicing John or his students. Luckily, the all-Black village of Robbins, Illinois, provided John and his student aviators land on which to build an airstrip and hanger.

Regrettably, months after the Robbins' facility was built, a rare spring storm demolished the new airplane hanger and the three planes it housed.

Having lost his plane, the year before in the Robbins' storm, John borrowed an aircraft to fly to his 10-year class reunion at Tuskegee Institute. In addition to spending time with his classmates, John planned to meet with the college's leadership concerning his desire to see the school provide aviation training. John was convinced that aviation could serve as a much-needed economic and social equalizer. Though, given that the country was in the middle of the Great Depression, Tuskegee's leadership was occupied with keeping the school financially stable and maintaining the programs they already offered. Economic and social equality would have to wait. Meanwhile, 7,000 miles away, the first strains of fascism were about to thrust John onto the world stage.

For generations of of African-Americans, the country of Ethiopia served as a touchstone of Black freedom, in part due to its centuries of independence and ancient Biblical roots. Since the 1500s, Ethiopia had defied Egyptian, Greek, Roman, Persian, and Muslim aggression and had remained an unconquered beacon of hope.

In the late 1890s, Italy's attempt to colonize a sovereign Ethiopia resulted in its suffering a humiliating defeat. Nearly 40 years later, Benito Mussolini, Italy's Fascist leader, was in a position to extract revenge against this great symbol of freedom. Strategically, Mussolini needed Ethiopia to fall in order for him to implement his grand plan of empire building across the Horn of Africa and Arabia.

While attending a luncheon with Chicago's Black business and civic leaders in January 1935, John publicly announced his intentions to defend Ethiopia as a military volunteer. Word of John's intentions reached Dr. Melaku Bayen, a cousin of Ethiopian Emperor Haile Selassie. After investigating John and his background, Dr. Bayen reported his findings to the Emperor. It was decided that the multi-talented aviator could best serve their cause by training pilots for Ethiopia's Imperial Air Force. Three months later, Emperor Haile Selassie officially offered John an officer's commission in Ethiopia's Imperial Air Force.

What John found upon his arrival in Ethiopia was an Air Force that existed mainly in Haile Selassie's mind. The Imperial Air Force consisted of a few pilots and a dozen antiquated planes in various stages of disrepair. There was a French Potez 25, a German Junker 52, and the Emperor's personal sports plane, an Italian Breda. As in his previous jobs, Robinson's duties increased once the extent of his knowledge became known. In a matter of weeks, John was promoted to the position of Commander of Ethiopia's Imperial Air Force. As Commander, John found himself responsible for all aspects of aviation operations, as he quickly busied himself with the preparation of his minuscule fleet of planes for war. Aside from his herculean attempts to acquire more airplanes, John held responsibility for aircraft repairs, maintenance, pilot training, and reconnaissance flying. In the end, John oversaw a fleet of 24 airplanes, of which only three would survive the war. Mussolini, on the other hand, had nearly 400 aircraft at his disposal.

From October 1935 to May 1936, Italy waged a merciless war on Ethiopia and her people. While the brave Ethiopians fought with spears, bows, and old rifles, Italian forces mowed down Ethiopian fighters with machine guns, armored tanks, and illegal mustard gas. For days the skies were abuzz with Italian grenades and bombs that battered both military and civilian targets. Even Red Cross facilities and ambulances were gassed. Two days before the fall of Addis Ababa, Ethiopia's capital, John, with Selassie's blessing, left his post and headed back to America. Though the act of securing passage back to America involved daring, split second timing, and lots of luck.

When John arrived in New York, he was considered a war hero and was accorded movie star treatment from both the press and Black America. Nicknamed *"The Brown Condor"* by the New York Times, John was cheered by adoring crowds and feted with banquets, parades, and other celebratory events. The flying ace was as popular as Olympian Jesse Owens and heavyweight boxing champion Joe Lewis!

After settling back into everyday life, John started his own flight school, but still longed to launch an aerospace program at his beloved Tuskegee. As hard as he tried, John's and Tuskegee's timing were never in sync, resulting in him not being involved with the Tuskegee Airmen Experiment, though he is sentimentally remembered as the Father of the Tuskegee Airmen.

John did however serve as an instructor at Keesler Airforce Base in Biloxi, Mississippi, during World War II before the Air Force bowed to Congressional pressure concerning a Black man instructing white pilots.

Soon after the Allied Forces drove Italy out of Ethiopia, John returned to Addis Ababa as an aviation asset in America's World War II lend-lease program. In addition to training pilots for Ethiopia's reconstituted Air Force, Robinson co-founded Sultan Airways, which would grow into Ethiopian Airlines.

Ten years after returning to Ethiopia, John died from burns he suffered as he rode the wind one last time. Carrying blood to a young boy injured by an airplane propeller, John's plane crashed into the Ethiopian mountainside. Although he never returned home or to Tuskegee Institute, his spirit still rides the wind with all those he inspired.

"Throughout history, it has been the inaction of those who could have acted, the indifference of those who should have known better, the silence of the voice of justice when it mattered most, that has made it possible for evil to triumph."

Haile Selassie I
Emperor of Ethiopia

John Charles Robinson

Public Domain Image.

John Charles Robinson
Audacity Principle: Preparedness

As a child, John Robinson did not belong to a Boy Scout troop, but he could have. He embodied the Scout motto—*Be Prepared*. He spent his free time in preparation for a career that, in all likelihood, only he saw as possible, much less probable. The passion of his life from age seven forward was aviation, and his enthusiasm for airplanes was all consuming.

John constantly talked about, dreamt about, and read about flying machines. As a teen, he excitedly consumed newspaper accounts of the mid-air dog fights and other exploits of World War I pilots. He was equally as awe struck by the trick flying of pioneering African-American aviatrix, Bessie Coleman. For John, it did not matter that the possibility or probability of a young Black man from the American South becoming an aviation standard bearer was near zero. John did everything he could to prepare for a future in aviation. Intuitively he understood that opportunities to fulfill his dream of flying would come through the act of preparation.

The more he interfaced with the world of aviation, the more he became familiar with the many paths that led to fulfillment in the air. There was design, repair, manufacturing, and air traffic control. There was military, civil, commercial, and private piloting opportunities. The more he prepared, the more opportunities presented themselves, even if he had to squeeze into the smallest of openings to get his foot in the door. Similar to Abraham Lincoln, John knew if he prepared, one day his chance would come.

John Robinson is a prime example of thought leader Trish Carr's dictum of "being known before you're needed." It is highly unlikely Ethiopian Emperor Haile Selassie would have extended an invitation for John to join him in his fight against Benito Mussolini if John's zeal for aviation had not been known and easily validated. Only an expert, not a novice, could accomplish in a matter of months what John achieved with Selassie's minuscule aviation assets.

What is it that you long for over the horizon? A split-level home, a dream vacation, a comfortable retirement? Without preparation, you probably will miss the mark of your desires. If you do not keep up to date with the changes in the economy and the amount of money needed to finance your plans or future lifestyle, you may unknowingly let your desire slip by. If you are not prepared, you cannot properly seize an opportunity, ideal or not. It is nearly impossible to make the most of that big break, if you are not prepared. Is any desire of your heart worthy of your time and attention if you do not see the value in preparing for its manifestation? If you take the time to think about your future, shouldn't you take the time to prepare for it? . As John demonstrated, one should be ready so there is no need to get ready when the opportunity presents itself

Only the audacious who prepare beforehand will find themselves in a position to snag the golden rings of opportunity, chance, or luck. Those who are not, will be left with dreams of what could have been. Which path will you choose?

"It is better to be prepared for an opportunity and not have one than to have an opportunity and not be prepared."

Whitney Moore Young, Jr.
Former Executive Director, National Urban League

John Charles Robinson Resources

BOOK
Father of the Tuskegee Airmen, John C. Robinson
Phillip Thomas Tucker
(Potomac Books, 2012)

ONLINE SITES
blackpast.org
selamtamagazine.com
usmilitariaforum.com

YOU TUBE VIDEO
MBE Stories C. John Robinson – The Ethiopian

SITES AND MEMORIALS TO VISIT
Mississippi Aviation Heritage Museum (opening 2020)
429 Pass Road
Gulfport, MS 39507

Commemorative Bust
Holy Trinity Cathedral
Addis Ababa, Ethiopia

John Robinson Reading Garden
United States Embassy
Addis Ababa, Ethiopia

Burial Site:
Ferenji Gulele Cemetery
Addis Ababa, Ethiopia

Dorie Miller
October 12, 1919–November 24, 1943

The year 1919 was not a good one for African-Americans. Hundreds were either injured or killed in anti-Black race riots that raged throughout the country. Scores of returning Black World War I veterans were subjected to public humiliation and physical abuse. Several were murdered while dressed in their military uniform. This also was the year the United States Navy barred Blacks from joining its ranks. Despite their history of commendable service, which began with the American Revolutionary War and continued through the first war to end all wars, Blacks would no longer be allowed to demonstrate their patriotism on the open seas.

Still, for Speegleville, Texas, sharecroppers Conery and Henrietta Miller, 1919 was a pretty good year. Contrary to the prediction of a local midwife that a baby girl would be joining her family of four, Henrietta Miller gave birth to a third son—Doris Miller. Eventually the new baby was nicknamed "Dorie."

For Japanese national, Isoroku Yamamoto, 1919 also proved to be a good year. Newly married, the 35-year-old Japanese naval officer earned the opportunity to study at America's most prestigious institution of higher education, Harvard University. When not studying, Isoroku learned the game of poker and became an obsessive player. A few years later as a member of Japan's diplomatic corps in Washington D.C., Isoroku spent a great deal of time playing poker with his American naval counterparts. From these interactions at the poker table, Isoroku concluded that the leadership of the U.S. Navy was soft and slow to react. This conclusion would years later inform the most pivotal decision of Isoroku's military career.

Down in Texas, life for the Miller family had stayed relatively the same. Most days were an exercise in survival. Similar to other share farmers, Conery and Henrietta Miller did not own the 28 acres on which they lived. The only possible way for them to break even, much less show a profit from their efforts, required every member of the family to shoulder their share of the work. School and education were luxuries that came after the planting and harvesting of crops. As a result, the family's third son, Dorie had only reached the eighth grade by the mid-1930s. When faced with having to repeat the eighth grade for the third time, Dorie decided to leave school and seek his fortune outside of Texas. Like many young men, Dorie thought the best way to achieve his goals was to join the Army, but he eventually enlisted in the Navy, which by this time was again accepting Black recruits. Little did Dorie know how events in his life would intersect with those masterminded by Harvard trained Japanese naval officer Isoroku Yamamoto.

Following completion of basic and ammunition support training, Dorie was assigned to the USS *West Virginia*, nicknamed the *WeeVee,* as a Mess Attendant Third Class. Just as general service ranks were off limits to Blacks, the Messman Branch was off limits to whites. Messmen were primarily Black, Filipino, or Chinese and were responsible for all activities related to eating—preparing and serving food, waiting tables, and washing dishes.

Although he held the lowest rank, which came with the lowest pay grade, Dorie did not forget about his family in Texas and regularly sent money home. To supplement his salary, Dorie also provided valet services such as laundry care and shoeshines to some of the ship's officers. For 22-year-old Dorie, this was living the life of his dreams.

Six thousand miles away from Dorie's boyhood home, the nation of Japan faced some of the same struggles the Miller family endured. During the early days of the 20th century, Japan was a relatively poor nation of 65 million that struggled to feed its people. With few natural resources, Japan relied on other countries for most of its food supply and the raw materials needed for its few industries. But in the 1930s Japan began to forcibly take what it needed from its neighbors. First it attacked Manchuria, then it declared war on China, and in 1940 it invaded French Indochina. To show its disapproval of Japan's aggression, the United States froze all Japanese assets on deposit in American banks and stopped the export of U.S. oil to the rogue nation.

Angered by American economic sanctions, Japan's leaders decided to unleash their wrath upon the United States. Isoroku Yamamoto who now was Marshal Admiral of the Imperial Japanese Navy (commander-in-chief of Japan's combined fleet) warned against this move. However, when his objections were overruled, Isoroku prepared for war.

Although at different points on their individual career ladders, neither Dorie Miller nor Isoroku Yamamoto knew that the other would eventually go down in history on opposing sides on a date destined to live in infamy.

On Sunday, December 7, 1941, the *USS West Virginia* was stationed in Hawaii's Pearl Harbor. That morning, Dorie worked the breakfast mess in the junior officers' dining room. Following a Saturday night of fun and relaxation, only two officers showed up for breakfast. Like most of the U.S. Pacific Fleet, the majority of the WeeVee's crew was still asleep. Having completed his assigned duties, Dorie moved on to his private valet services. With little warning, the calm of the morning was broken by the urgent and thundering announcement "Away Fire and Rescue Party," naval code for rescue squad needed to assist with an accident away from the ship. Within seconds, a scream of "General Quarters" was made—also known as the call for everyone to report to their assigned battle stations as quickly as possible.

Japan had declared war on America.

Neither Dorie nor any of his shipmates were aware that the skies were filled with the first wave of Japanese aircrafts loaded with torpedoes, bombs, and bullets intent on avenging American economic sanctions that had nearly dried up the flow of oil to the oil-dependent nation.

Dorie Miller-Public Domain Wikipedia

When Dorie reached his below-deck battle station, he found it in ruins, destroyed by a Japanese torpedo. As he rushed up to the main deck to report himself available for other duty, a scorching piece of hot metal debris from the *USS Tennessee* tore open the stomach of his Captain, Mervyn Bennion. After he assisted in carrying the Captain to safety, Dorie was ordered to pass ammunition to two anti-aircraft gunners. In an instant, one of the gun operators was cut down. At that point, Dorie took charge of his wounded shipmate's .50-caliber anti-aircraft machine gun.

Without hesitation, Dorie loaded the gun and began to fire the hulking *widow maker*. For fifteen minutes, Dorie fired at anything moving in the sky until he ran out of bullets. The exact number of enemy planes Miller shot down is unknown, with estimates ranging from zero to six. Dorie then began to pull his fellow sailors out of the burning harbor waters and continued to do so until the final order to abandon ship was given. Even after the abandon order, Miller was one of the last three people to leave the sinking vessel.

Despite the heroic efforts of many, when the final Japanese airplane turned back to the Land of the Rising Sun, 2,403 Americans were dead and another 1,143-lay wounded.

Initially Dorie's heroics were attributed to an unnamed Negro. But after months of agitation from the Black press and shrewd detective work by historian Dr. Lawrence Reddick, curator of the Schomburg Collection of Negro Literature at the New York Public Library, Dorie was identified as the unnamed Negro and heralded as a hero. He was also sent back to his mop and broom.

After more public outcries for recognition of his valor, on May 27, 1942, Dorie received the second highest naval award for his selfless acts of courage—the Navy Cross. He was also promoted to Mess Attendant First Class. Later that year, he was dispatched to several cities on a war bond tour and was reunited with his family when the tour brought him to Texas. When asked his thoughts during the attack on Pearl Harbor, Dorie replied, "When the Japanese bombers attacked my ship…I forgot about the fact that I and other Negroes can only be Messmen in the Navy and are not taught how to man an anti-aircraft gun."

On April 18, 1943, while Dorie was still on his war bond tour, the United States military set in motion its plan to kill Marshal Admiral Isoroku Yamamoto, architect of the Pearl Harbor massacre. The mission, known by its code name Operation Vengeance, called for American bombers to shoot down the plane carrying Isoroku on an inspection tour of Japanese bases in the South Pacific near Bougainville Island. When the wreckage from his plane was located, the dead Admiral was found under a tree, still in his seat, sitting upright gripping his sword.

Six weeks after the completion of his successful fundraising tour, Dorie received another promotion and was assigned to the escort carrier *USS Liscome Bay*. Tragically during the early morning hours of November 24, 1943, as its crew was preparing for the carrier's first combat mission, a torpedo from Japanese submarine *I-175* struck the ship's bomb magazine. In less than 25 minutes, the carrier sunk with only 272 members of its crew of more than 900 surviving. Dorie was not one of the survivors.

The following year the Navy graduated its first Black general service officers—the Golden 13. In many ways Dorie's unselfish response to duty was one of the catalysts that made possible the integration of the Navy's officer ranks.

Though he lay in a watery grave, Dorie Miller's selfless devotion to his fellow man and country remains as strong now as it was December 7th, 1941. Dorie's heroism continues on in the honorable service and valor of today's African-American naval admirals, officers, and enlisted men.

###

"The brave man is not he who does not feel afraid, but he who conquers that fear."

Nelson Mandela
Former President of South Africa and Anti-Apartheid Revolutionary

Doris "Dorie" Miller
Audacity Principle: Bravery

Blacks have served with honor and dignity in every American military conflict. Starting with the 1715–1716 Yamasee War, Blacks proudly bore arms as a demonstration of their loyalty, faithfulness, and allegiance to America and the democratic principles she represents. More than 5,000 Blacks fought against the British in the American Revolution. An undetermined number answered the call to arms in the War of 1812, and roughly 198,000 served in the Union Army and Navy during the Civil War. Following the war, fourteen Black Union soldiers were awarded the Congressional Medal of Honor for various acts of valor.

In the Spanish-American, Mexican-American, Philippine-American, and the first World Wars, Black soldiers exhibited the same bravery, heroism, and fearlessness of their forefathers. Still, in 1925, the United States Army sought to codify the bias, bigotry, and prejudice Black soldiers had campaigned so hard to dispel.

In a 1925 Army War College study that purportedly was an examination of the fitness of Black soldiers for service in future wars, the following three excerpts speak volumes:

1. *"The American negro has not progressed as far as the other sub-species of the human family. As a race he has not developed leadership qualities. His mental inferiority and the inherent weaknesses of his character are factors that must be considered with great care in the preparation of any plan for his employment in war ... ."*

2. *"It is generally recognized that the pure blood American negro is inferior to our white population in mental capacity ... . The cranial cavity of the negro is smaller than the white; his brain weighing 35 ounces contrasted with 45 for the white."*

3. *"All officers, without exception, agree that the Negro lacks initiative, displays little or no leadership, and cannot accept responsibility. Some point out that these defects are greater in the Southern Negro ... ."*

Six years before the Army War College report, the United States Navy refused to enlist any more Blacks for naval service. When the Navy did re-open its doors to young Black men like Dorie Miller, it did not allow them to serve in combat or leadership roles. Their skills and talents were relegated to bath and laundry rooms and ship kitchens. But Dorie's multiple acts of bravery, courage, and selflessness at Pearl Harbor were indisputable evidence that Blacks were as courageous, gallant, and brave as the next military man.

Fortunately, most people do not often find themselves in life or death situations that call for herculean bravery. However, each day you are presented with countless opportunities to choose bravery as your default audacity principle. For example, you can choose to stand up for any number of social injustices that may make others uncomfortable, such as health care inequality or access to quality education options for all children regardless of their zip code. Or you may choose to fight for or against issues that do not make the list of polite conversation. Examples of inappropriate or explosive topics include capital punishment or immigration policy. Utilization of your mental and moral strength is just as important and necessary, as physical power, during times of environmental peril and adversity.

Bravery is not limited to outward acts or oriented only toward others. Life presents numerous chances to either stand tall or shrink away. Are you brave enough to go back to school and earn that college degree you started twenty years ago? Can you hold your own hand as you work to transition from a dead-end job into the career of your dreams? Do you have the audacity to ask for more meaningful work assignments or that raise you were promised two years ago?

Bravery is not the absence of fear, it is the acceptance of fear and a willingness to move forward in spite of it. It is your choice to become a victim of circumstances, conditions, and situations or to become a pioneer of new latitudes, possibilities, and options. Fear is present in each choice, but it is up to you to choose the opportunity with the more meaningful return.

"Bravery is not the absence of fear, it is overcoming it."

Mellody Hobson
President and Co-CEO of Ariel Investments

Doris "Dorie" Miller Resources

BOOKS
Dorie Miller-Hero of Pearl Harbor
Bill O. Neil
(Eakin Press, 2007)

Grade Levels: 5-7
Greatness Under Fire
Dante R. Brizill
(Kindle Direct Publisher, 2018)

ONLINE SITES
atomicheritage.org/
history.com
newyorktimes.com
usswestvirginia.org
washingtontpost.com

YOU TUBE VIDEOS
The Story Behind an American Hero, Ship's Mess Attendant Doris Miller
Remembering Pearl Harbor: Dorie Miller

SITES AND MEMORIALS TO VISIT
Doris Miller Memorial
300 N. Martin Luther King Jr. Blvd.
Waco, TX 76704

Pearl Harbor Visitor Center
1 Arizona Memorial Place
Honolulu, HI 96818

12. CANTALOUPE

Mamie "Peanut" Johnson
September 27, 1935–December 18, 2017

Ten-year-old Mamie Johnson was in love. Mamie had been introduced to the object of her affection by her uncle Leo. When school or chores separated Mamie from her passion, she eagerly looked forward to their next date. Regardless of what others said, Mamie knew that her devotion would last a lifetime. What could bring forth such strong emotions in a young girl? Well, it was not a boy! It was the game of baseball or, more specifically, the ball itself.

Mamie, an only child, was born in rural Ridgeway, South Carolina during the mid-years of The Great Depression. She lived with her grandmother, Cendonia, and her uncle, Leo, who was just a few years older than her, while her mother worked as a dietician in Washington, D.C. Like most children, Mamie spent as much time as she could outdoors roaming her grandmother's 81-acre homestead. When she was not doing chores, she ruled the roost of her makeshift baseball diamond.

On her field, an old pie plate served as first base, while a flowerpot fragment served as second. Third base was a large protruding tree root, and home plate was marked by a lid from a five-gallon bucket of King Cane syrup. When Mamie could not borrow a baseball from her school, she made her own. After finding a suitable rock, Mamie would build her ball by layering it in tape until she achieved the desired thickness and weight. Her bat was any strong branch that she could hoist up to smack oncoming balls.

Mamie's love for baseball shown brightest as she stood in the middle of her ballpark. Under her uncle's watchful eye, Mamie's love continued to grow and mature. Always a willing student, Mamie was both coachable and a star. Along with her ability to size up a batter's shortcomings, Mamie was a power pitcher whose balls sliced through the air with accuracy and precision. She could read the weaknesses of most batters, which helped her deliver the right pitch at the right time. Her love affair with the nine-inch ball was not puppy love. It was the real thing.

Grandma Cendonia's death temporarily forced Mamie from her perch atop the pitcher's mound. Without anyone to care for Mamie while her mother worked to establish a home for them in Washington, D. C., Mamie moved to Long Branch, New Jersey, to live with another aunt and uncle. Although she now lived in a city with lots of buildings, stores, and parks, there was no baseball team for girls. To try and ease Mamie's loss of her beloved baseball kingdom, her uncle gave her a catcher's mitt and fielded the ball with her whenever he could. Her aunt signed her up for girls' softball. After three games, Mamie was AWOL.

The nicest thing she ever said about softball was that the size of the ball reminded her of a cantaloupe. One afternoon as she slow-poked her way back to her aunt and uncle's home, Mamie spied a group of young white boys playing baseball. Her attempts at complimenting their skills opened up a flow of sexist and racist comments that only ended when their coach, police officer Campbell, appeared on the scene. Campbell told Mamie that the team was a part of the Police Athletic League and only those with the best skills were chosen to play. That was all Mamie needed to hear. The next day, Mamie showed up at the police station ready for a tryout. Not only did Mamie show Officer Campbell she was one of the best, she went on to lead his boys to two divisional championships.

By the late 1940s America's pastime was changing. Jackie Robinson had broken baseball's color line and the newest technology, television, had moved the game from the ballpark to fans' living rooms. Having reunited with her mother in Washington, D.C., Mamie realized that more women were swinging bats and hitting baseballs, as she continued to hone her skills with the guys. From spring to early fall, Mamie fired off sliders, grounders, and knuckle balls as a pitcher with the St. Cyprian men's recreational athletic league of Washington D.C. But Mamie wanted more and thought she might get it with the All-American Girls Professional Baseball League (AAGPBL).

Baseball big wigs like Branch Rickey, manager of the Brooklyn Dodgers, and Philip K. Wrigley, chewing gum heir and owner of the Chicago Cubs, were two of AAGPBL's strongest backers. Due to the large number of professional men's baseball players who were fighting in World War II, baseball management was faced with the real prospect of half-empty stadiums. The AAGPBL was organized as a defensive move to cushion the financial shortfalls caused by the war. After the war's end, the AAGPBL remained active and was looking for new players. Maybe the AAGPBL could turn Mamie's dreams of playing in the big leagues into reality. It did not.

Unlike Officer Campbell of the police athletic league, the man in charge of the AAGPBL's All-American's tryout did not allow Mamie's feet to touch the diamond, much less give her a tryout. It was 1947 when Jackie Robinson crossed Major League Baseball's male color line, but its female league, with its Blacks-need-not-apply policy, happily continued snuffing out the professional league dreams of talented African-American female baseball players.

If Mamie thought elementary school softball was a romp in powder-puff femininity, she would have died a quick death in the AAGPBL. Players were required to take etiquette and make-up classes, keep their hair long, and wear lipstick at all times. Perhaps if more attention would have been paid to the quality of its games versus the looks of its players, the league may have survived. Within a year of Mamie's fruitless encounter with the AAGPBL, it was out of business.

Mamie quickly rebounded from the AAGPBL's snub and continued to hone her skills with the St. Cyprian men's league. Eventually her skills were noticed by someone who could advance her career, Bish Tyson. He had come to Mamie's last few games, but to Mamie he was just another cheering fan. Bish, however, was a scout on a mission to find a special female player for the male dominated Negro League's Indianapolis Clowns. Perhaps Mamie was that player.

After he introduced himself, Bish invited Mamie to try out for the Miami Clowns. The club had started out as the Miami Giants a few years before Mamie's birth. Known as a two-for-one team, the Clowns played good baseball and entertained fans with routines that had ranged from the worst elements of minstrel comedy to acceptable family-friendly fare. In the team's infancy, players pretended to be African savages who smeared their faces with war paint and dressed in grass skirts. Over time the team's antics relied more on slapstick and physical comedy routines. From pretending to play invisible baseball to pulling teeth, the Clowns were a crowd favorite. They also played great baseball.

For once, a team had come to Mamie with an offer to play real professional baseball. Would she make the cut? Absolutely. With a newly inked contract, seventeen-year-old Mamie headed to Portsmouth, Virginia, for spring training.

Mamie was not the first female to sign on with the Clowns. That honor belonged to Toni Stone. Born as Marcenia Lyle Stone in Bluefield, West Virginia, the 32-year-old Toni started her professional baseball career with the San Francisco Sea Lions. Her sweet spot was second base, the position former Clown player Willie Mays held the year prior to her joining the team.

Once Mamie showed off her ball-handling skills and abilities, her male teammates felt she was worthy of a spot on the team roster. The team's 150-game schedule was a mixture of league and barnstorming or exhibition play. Their season was baseball's version of the Chitlin' Circuit—a patchwork of small towns and big cities throughout the South, the East Coast, and the Midwest that tolerated Black entertainment. During any given week, the Clowns might play games against recreational leagues, white semi-pro teams, or rag-tag neighborhood squads. The quality of play also ranged from competitive to shameful. Regardless of the team the Clowns played, there was one unifying aim—winning. If the team won a game, they received 60% of the gate. When they lost, their payout was only 40%. When it came to winning games, fun and foolishness took a back seat.

Mamie did her part to keep the team in the black. She could make any ball humble the arrogant, unnerve the timid, or sing her praises on command. Mamie was a solid player the Clowns could count on. When she faced off against Kansas City Monarchs' infielder Hank Baylis, Mamie proved to him and all present why the pitching mound was her throne. When Baylis roared to the crowd "That little girl's no bigger than a peanut. I ain't afraid of her," Mamie proceeded to strike him out. From that point forward, Mamie was "Peanut." During her professional career, Mamie posted an 80-20 win-loss ratio. Not bad for a peanut.

Between seasons, Mamie got married and gave birth to a son. As much as she loved being a professional baseball player, her son's heartbreaking reactions to her long absences led Mamie back home to motherhood and a career in nursing. But for three years, Mamie "Peanut" Johnson lived her best life as the only female pitcher to ever take the mound in professional men's baseball.

"With confidence, you have won before you have started."

Marcus Garvey
Jamaican Political Activist

Mamie "Peanut" Johnson

Image courtesy of the Negro Leagues Baseball Museum, Inc.

Mamie "Peanut" Johnson
Audacity Principle: Confidence

Tomboy. Unladylike. Too rough. Mamie "Peanut" Johnson heard it all, and it did not bother her one bit. She did not worry about what others thought. She felt good about who she was and what she was able to accomplish with a five-ounce baseball. From scattering birds sitting on her grandmother's fence line with her powerful pitches, to mowing down formidable male competitors, Mamie was confident in her abilities to play with the best. She was an all-around good player and an excellent pitcher. It also did not hurt that as a young girl her athletic abilities were not limited by the adults in her life. Mamie was never presented with a list of off-limit and unacceptable gender-based behaviors.

Having confidence in or feeling sure about your abilities is an audacious trait that can be learned and utilized for the benefit of yourself and others. For starters, you must trust in your own capabilities to get the job done. You must know that you can, even if you haven't yet. You may not hit a home run your first time at bat, but even if you walk the bases, you are gaining ground. Each time you complete a task related to your goals; you are building up confidence.

Also, do not buy into the noise of detractors. Once you lock in on your goals, such as learning a new language, being elected to the local school board, or improving your health through increased physical activity, do not let the doubts, misgivings, and qualms of others stop your progress. Replace their limiting jabber with affirming self-talk. Famed advertising executive Bruce Barton was correct when he noted that "*nothing splendid has ever been achieved except by those who believe that something inside of them was superior to the situation.*"

Which brings us to the next point. Know your stuff! When you spend more time improving your knowledge base, skill set, talents, and gifts, you become more self-assured. This does not mean becoming a know-it-all. It does mean spending time learning and, when appropriate, sharing what you have learned with others. As thought leader Nancy Matthews encourages, we should strive to "Be the One" that makes the difference in the lives of others. The difference may be as simple and pleasant as offering a smile of confidence to the new cashier at the drugstore, or as complex as finding the courage to tell your best friend her bad breath may be turning off would-be suitors. In most every instance, confidence requires a dose of courage.

Finally, you may need to profess confidence until your own positive concepts of who you truly are take root. Sometimes we have to *act as if.* If you think you are executive material, you are. Act like an executive. This does not mean trading in your minivan for a chauffeured limousine, but it does mean that your stride should reflect self-assurance, your speech should have the ring of authority, and your actions should demonstrate proficiency. The more you profess it, the sooner you will confess it. If you want to play in the major leagues, you must leave your fears, doubts, and worries with the farm team. For only the confident, bold, and fearless become world champions.

"It's lack of faith that makes people afraid of meeting challenges, and I believed in myself."

Muhammad Ali
Former Heavyweight Boxing Champion of the World

Mamie "Peanut" Johnson Resources

BOOK
Grade Levels 4-7:
A Strong Right Arm: The Story of Mamie "Peanut" Johnson
Michelle Y. Green
(Puffin Books; Reprint edition 2004)

ONLINE SITES
aaregistry.org
encyclopedia.com
https://baseballhall.org/npr.org
originalpeople.org
thenewyorktimes.com

YOU TUBE VIDEOS
Hidden Figures: Mamie 'Peanut' Johnson #BlackHERstoryMonth
Mamie "Peanut" Johnson: Joining The Negro Leagues
On the Shoulders of Giants Channel: Mamie "Peanut" Johnson

SITES AND MEMORIALS TO VISIT
Mamie "Peanut" Johnson Field
Rosedale Community Center
Washington, D. C.

Burial Site:
Washington National Cemetery
Suitland, MD

AUDACITY TIMELINE

1619	Twenty enslaved Africans arrive in Jamestown, Virginia.
1662	Virginia law decrees children born in the colony assume their mother's social status contrary to English common law which endowed children with their father's standing. Children born to enslaved mothers were automatically enslaved.
1744	Elizabeth "MumBet" Freeman born in Claverack, New York.
1776–1783	5,000 free blacks in the American North fight alongside the colonists during the American Revolution.
1781	Enslaved Elizabeth"MumBet" Freeman sues for and wins her freedom in the Massachusetts Courts.
1787	Delegates to the United States' Constitutional Convention decide for the purpose of taxation and representation, enslaved African-Americans would be counted as 3/5th of a person.
1806	Inventor Norbert Rillieux born in New Orleans, Louisiana.
1807	Shakespearian actor Ira Frederick Aldridge born in New York, New York.
1808	Congress bans further importation of slaves.
1833	Carriage maker Charles Richard Patterson born in Virginia.
1843	Norbert Rillieux receives first of two American patents for multiple-effect evaporator techniques.
1857	Dred Scott v. Sandford the landmark Supreme Court decision which stated the rights and privileges of American citizenship did not apply to free or enslaved African-Americans.
1859	Champion agriculturist Junius George Groves born in Green County, Kentucky.

1861–1865	American Civil War-roughly 198,000 African-Americans served in the Union Army and Navy.
1861	Isaac Burns Murphy born in Fayette County Kentucky.
1863	Abraham Lincoln's Emancipation Proclamation proclaims that all slaves in rebellious territories are forever free.
1865	Southern states pass "Black Code Laws" which limited African-American freedoms.
1866	Polar Explorer Matthew Alexander Henson born in Nanjemoy, Maryland.
1868	Ratification of 14th Amendment to U.S. Constitution which grants citizenship and equal rights to African-Americans.
1871	Automaker Frederick Douglass Patterson born in Greenfield, Ohio.
1881	First "Jim Crow" or racial segregation laws passed in Tennessee.
1883	United States Supreme Court overturns the Civil Rights Act of 1875 and declares the Federal Government cannot prohibit individuals or organizations from practicing racial discrimination.
1890	Magazine editor Lyda Moore Merrick is born in Durham, North Carolina.
1892	Celebrity Chef Lena Richard is born in New Road, Louisiana.
1896	Plessey v. Ferguson landmark United States Supreme Court decision that upheld the practice of racial separation in public facilities.
1905	Aviator John Charles Robinson born in Carrabelle, Florida.
1919	World War II hero Doris "Dorie" Miller born in Speegleville, Texas.
1920	First national African-American baseball league founded.
1921	Disability activist John Carter Washington born in Durham, North Carolina.
1935	Professional baseball player Mamie "Peanut" Johnson born in Ridgeway, South Carolina.

1941   Surprise Japanese military attack on United States naval fleet in Pearl Harbor, Hawaii.

1948   Lena Richard's New Orleans Cook Book debuts on New Orleans television station WDSU.

1954   Brown v. Board of Education landmark United States Supreme Court decision which declared racially segregated schools unconstitutional.

CPSIA information can be obtained
at www.ICGtesting.com
Printed in the USA
LVHW032238190221
679369LV00005B/324